True Worship

by
John MacArthur, Jr.

Library of Congress Cataloging-in-Publication Data

MacArthur, John F.
    True worship.

    (John MacArthur's Bible studies)
    1. Public worship   2. Public worship—Biblical
teaching.   I. Title   II. Series: MacArthur, John F.
Bible studies.
BV15.M23 1985   264   85-25912
ISBN 0-8024-5108-X (pbk.)

ISBN: 0-8024-5108-X

1 2 3 4 5 6 7 Printing/GB/Year 90 89 88 87 86 85

Printed in the United States of America

Contents

1

True Worship—Part 1

Outline

Introduction
A. Worship Defined
B. Worship Depicted
    1. The fragrance of the Tabernacle's incense
    2. The fragrance of Mary's ointment
C. Worship Distinguished

Lesson
I. The Importance of Worship
  A. Scripture Is Dominated with It
    1. Old Testament passages
      a) The emphasis of the first commandment (Ex. 20)
      b) The establishment of the Tabernacle (Ex. 25)
      c) The encampment around the Tabernacle (Num. 1:52—2:2)
      d) The example of the seraphim (Isa. 6:1-2)
      e) The exhortation of the psalmist (Ps. 95:6-7*a*)
    2. New Testament passages
      a) Romans 12:1-2
      b) 1 Peter 2:5
  B. Destiny Is Determined by It
    1. Unacceptable worship
      a) The worship of false gods
        (1) Earthly/material gods
        (2) Heavenly/supernatural gods

Introduction

John 4:20-24 is going to be the touchstone for our study of worship. We'll be coming back to it intermittently throughout this series, and then we'll look at it in more depth. I believe John 4:20-24 is the most significant New Testament passage on the subject of worship—so we must understand its truths.

Our text is a conversation between the woman of Samaria and our Lord Jesus Christ. She says, "Our fathers worshiped in this mountain; and ye say that in Jerusalem is the place where men ought to *worship*. Jesus saith unto her, Woman, believe me, the hour cometh, when ye shall neither in this mountain, nor yet at Jerusalem, *worship* the Father. Ye *worship* ye know not what. We know what we *worship*; for salvation is of the Jews. But the hour cometh, and now is, when the true worshipers shall *worship* the Father in spirit and in truth; for the Father seeketh such to *worship* him. God is a Spirit; and they that *worship* him must *worship* him in spirit and in truth" (italics added). The word "worship" appears eight times in this passage. Therefore, it is essential that we understand what our Lord is saying here.

Most people go to church for what they can get. Some people just check out the church page in their newspaper to see who's playing where on a given Sunday, and go for what will appeal to them or "bless" them. Well, if you go to church for what you can *get* out of the music, or what you can *get* out of the sermon, or just to *get* blessed, you've missed the point. The music and the sermon aren't ends in themselves, they are but stimuli to cause you to worship God. And if you have any thought less than that, you've missed the point!

We go to church to worship God, and that's done by giving, not getting. We go to offer something to Him, not to receive from Him. Granted, if we offer to Him the praise due His name, we will receive at His hand. There is blessing in giving, for the Lord is quoted as saying, "It is more blessed to give than to receive" (Acts 20:35*b*). So, worship is giving to God, not getting.

Do you worship when you go to church? Is that what's in your mind? Do you prepare your heart for worship? When you are getting dressed, or when you are in your car on your way to church, is your heart eager to worship God? Have you ever asked yourself these questions? Well, if you haven't, I'm going to force you to do so in these chapters. In fact, my purpose is to force you to make a decision about whether you're going to worship God or not. My objective is to make you think, first of all, about what worship is; second, whether you're doing it or not; and third, if not—will you? And if you won't, then you're going to have to deny what the Bible says. I want to force you into a corner where you have no other alternative than to do what God says, or not do what God says, and know clearly what you've done.

A. Worship Defined

What is worship? Let me give you a definition: *Worship is "honor paid to a superior being."* It means "to give homage, honor, reverence, respect, adoration, praise, or glory to a superior being." In Scripture, the word is used indiscriminately to refer to the homage given to idols, material things, or to the true God. So the word in itself is not a holy word, it only describes honor given to a superior being.

The common New Testament word for worship is *proskuneō*, which means "to kiss toward, to kiss the hand, to bow down, to prostrate oneself." The idea of worship is that one prostrates himself before a superior being with a sense of respect, awe, reverence, honor, and homage. In a Christian context, we simply apply this to God. We bow before God and prostrate ourselves before Him in respect and honor, paying Him the glory due His superior character.

Essentially, then, worship is giving—giving honor and respect to God. That is why we, as Christians, gather together on Sunday. We don't gather to give respect to the preacher or those in the choir, we gather to give honor to God. The sermon and the music are just to be the stimuli that create the desire in our hearts to honor Him.

So, if you attend church for what you can get (i.e., to "get a blessing"), you've missed it! When we gather together to worship the Lord, our focus is to be on giving *to* Him, not getting *from* Him. Worship is a consuming desire to give to God, and it involves the giving of ourselves, our heart attitudes, and our possessions.

B. Worship Depicted

Let me illustrate this idea of worship.

1. The fragrance of the Tabernacle's incense

Exodus 30:34-38 provides a graphic illustration of worship. God gave many instructions regarding how worship was to be carried out in the Tabernacle. Many of the instructions had great symbolic value and were used as teaching tools. One of these visual aids, described in Exodus 30:34-38, gives us a wonderful insight into the area of worship:

"And the Lord said unto Moses, Take unto thee sweet spices, stacte, and onycha, and galbanum; these sweet spices with pure frankincense: of each shall there be a like weight: And thou shalt make it a perfume, a perfume after the art of the perfumer, tempered together, pure and holy [i.e., unique, separate, and untouched by any other elements]: And thou shalt beat some of it very small, and put of it before the testimony in the tabernacle of the congregation, where I will meet with thee: it shall be unto you most holy."

Now this perfume, which was actually a sweet-smelling incense, was to be used only in the Tabernacle. Why? Because it was to be holy. Verse 37 continues, "And as for the perfume which thou shalt make, ye shall not make to yourselves according to the composition thereof: it shall be unto thee holy for the Lord. Whosoever shall make like unto that, to smell thereto, shall even be cut off from his people." Now, did you know there was a perfume recipe in the Bible? It was probably the most lovely fragrance imaginable, but God said that it could cost them their lives if they made it for themselves.

You say, "Well, what's the point?" The point is this: here was a fragrance designed to be only for God. When this incense rose to God's nostrils, it was unique to Him. This is a beautiful picture of worship, showing that worship is to be a unique, separated, sanctified, holy act that rises out of a person's heart to the very nostrils of God.

2. The fragrance of Mary's ointment

As the fragrance of the incense in the Tabernacle rose to the nostrils of God, it signified worship. In John 12:1-3, another fragrant gift is offered in worship. However, this time it was offered to the living God in human form—the Lord Jesus Christ:

9

"Then Jesus, six days before the passover, came to Bethany, where Lazarus was, who had been dead, whom he raised from the dead. There they made him a supper, and Martha served; but Lazarus was one of them that sat at the table with him. Then took Mary a pound of ointment of spikenard, very costly [probably a year's wages], and anointed the feet of Jesus, and wiped his feet with her hair; and the house was filled with the odor of the ointment." Mary used that which was her glory, her hair (cf. I Cor. 11:15), to wash the dusty, dirty feet of Jesus. And she didn't use water; she used a costly, fragrant ointment. That's the essence of worship. It's self-humiliating and profuse in its giving.

Mary and Martha were different. Martha was always serving, and Mary was always sitting at the feet of Jesus. In fact, Jesus had previously said that what Mary chose to do was better than all of Martha's serving (cf. Lk. 10:38-42). But when Judas saw what Mary did with the ointment, he said, "Why was not this ointment sold for three hundred denarii, and given to the poor?" (v. 5). Verse 6 tells us that Judas didn't really care about the poor, he just wanted the money for himself. So Jesus said to him, "Let her alone. . . . For the poor always ye have with you, but me ye have not always" (vv. 7a, 8). In other words, it's better to worship than to give welfare. What we give God is infinitely more important than what we give to man—any man. Now I'm not saying that it's not important to give to our fellow man, but it's *more* important to give to God.

We tend to be so pragmatic, don't we? We are a generation of Marthas—always busy. We have the church fine-tuned to a system, with all of its programs and activities. And we are very careful not to waste our substance; so much so, that even what we give to God we tend to mark out very carefully, rather than to pour out that which is a year's wages and to stoop in humility to wipe His feet with our hair.

Mary's act was an act of true worship. As the fragrance rose from her ointment, it portrayed the essence of a worshiping heart. That's what God is after. True worship is better than welfare and religious activity. Although those things are necessary and good, worship is better. And yet, I fear that many of us don't even know what worship is.

C. Worship Distinguished

I think a comparison of worship with ministry might help to distinguish what true worship really is. Ministry is that which *comes down* to us from the Father, through the Son, in the power of the Spirit, to one another in the form of spiritual gifts. Worship, on the other hand, is that which *goes up* from us, by the Spirit's power, through the Son, to the Father. Thus, ministry is that which *descends* from God to us, while worship is that which *ascends* from us to God. And both must be in perfect balance. Unfortunately, we tend to be too ministry oriented (like Martha) and not oriented enough toward worship. We need to learn from Mary how to sit at Jesus' feet and worship Him.

Ask yourself the following questions: "Do I worship God? Is worship a priority for me? Do I faithfully and regularly attend church with a deep heart commitment to worship God? Am I so consumed with a hungering desire to worship God that I hurry myself into the assembly of His people for the expression of worship?" Well, God seeks acceptable, true, spiritual worship, and if we're going to give it to Him, we must understand what it is.

Lesson

I. THE IMPORTANCE OF WORSHIP

A. Scripture Is Dominated with It

The first reason worship is important is because Scripture speaks so frequently of it. The Word of God emphasizes the theme of worship hundreds and hundreds of times, but I just want to pick out a few select passages to illustrate its priority.

1. Old Testament passages

    a) The emphasis of the first commandment (Ex. 20)

    When God began to lay down some standards, principles, and guidelines in the form of commandments, statutes, ordinances, laws, and propositions, what was it that was most important to Him? Notice the first commandment that He gave. "I am the Lord thy God, who have brought thee out of the land of Egypt, out the house of bondage. Thou shalt have no other gods before me. Thou shalt not make unto thee any carved image, or any likeness of anything that is in heaven above, or that is in the earth beneath, or that is in the water under the earth; thou shalt not bow down thyself to them, nor serve them; for I, the Lord thy God, am a jealous God, visiting the iniquity of the fathers upon the children unto the third and fourth generation of them that hate me; and showing mercy unto thousands of them that love me, and keep my commandments" (vv. 2-6). The first commandment, then, is to worship God and God alone. That is our priority (cf. Ex. 34:14; Matt. 22:37).

    b) The establishment of the Tabernacle (Ex. 25)

    When God called His people out of Egypt and they began to wander in the wilderness, He wanted them to focus on worshiping Him, so He established a place for this worship to occur—the Tabernacle. To give you an idea of the priority that God put on this place of worship, consider that it took seven chapters (a total of 243 verses) for God to discuss all the standards, measurements, and furnishings that were to be a part of the Tabernacle, and it only took thirty-one verses to describe the whole creation of the universe.

11

The Tabernacle itself was not very attractive, but inside the holy of holies, which was inside the holy place, was the ark of the covenant. On top of the ark was the mercy seat, where the high priest sprinkled blood once a year as an atonement for the sins of the people. It was on this mercy seat that the Shekinah glory of God dwelt, or tabernacled. In Exodus 25:22 God tells Moses, "And there will I meet with thee, and I will commune with thee from above the mercy seat, from between the two cherubim which are upon the ark of the testimony, of all things which I will give thee in commandment unto the children of Israel." God gave them the Tabernacle as a focal point of worship because worship was the priority.

c) The encampment around the Tabernacle (Num. 1:52—2:2)

It's interesting to see how God arranged the encampment of Israel during the forty years of wandering. Every time the children of Israel stopped to set up camp, the priests were to be closest to the Tabernacle; just beyond the priests were the Levites; the twelve tribes made up the outer ring. Now the priests were in charge of worship, while the other Levites were in charge of the service, the caring of the Tabernacle. It's obvious that the priority was that of worship.

Even the age requirement for a priest showed the importance of worship. When a young man reached the age of twenty, he could serve as a soldier (Num. 1:3). A Levite could begin to serve the Tabernacle when he reached the age of twenty-five (Num. 8:24). But a Levite had to be thirty before he could become a priest (Num. 4:3). Why? Because worship was the priority. It demanded the highest level of spiritual maturity because it was the greatest responsibility. There was one level for those who fought the battles and another for those who served in the Tabernacle—but the highest level was for those who brought the people to worship God.

d) The example of the seraphim (Isa. 6:1-2)

In Isaiah 6:1-2 Isaiah says, "In the year that King Uzziah died, I saw also the Lord sitting upon a throne, high and lifted up, and his train filled the temple. Above it stood the seraphim: each one had six wings; with two he covered his face, and with two he covered his feet, and with two he did fly." It's interesting that four of the wings were related to worship, and only two were related to service. Each one of the seraphim covered his face because he couldn't look upon God's glory, he covered his feet because of God's holy presence, and with the remaining two wings he took care of the service. Worship is the priority—even for the angels.

e) The exhortation of the psalmist (Ps. 95:6-7a)

Psalm 95:6-7a says, "Oh, come, let us worship and bow down; let us kneel before the Lord our maker. For he is our God."

This is just one of the many such Psalms which exhort us to worship (cf. Pss. 5:7; 29:2; 45:11; 66:4; 86:9; 96:9; 99:5, 9; 132:7; 138:2).

2. New Testament passages

    a) Romans 12:1-2

    In the first eleven chapters of Romans, Paul talks about the marvelous gospel of the Lord Jesus Christ, His redemptive purpose and plan for the world, and His mercy on sinful man. Then he says, "I beseech you therefore, brethren, by the mercies of God [all the truths of the first eleven chapters], that ye present your bodies a living sacrifice, holy acceptable unto God, which is your reasonable service [lit., 'spiritual worship']" (v. 1).

    Now, after eleven chapters of doctrine defining the Christian and all of his benefits, Paul says, "In response to all of this, God wants something from you." Do you know what it is? Spiritual worship which is acceptable to Him. The word "acceptable" is an important word of sacrifice and worship. Anyone who worships seeks to bring God that which is acceptable. This word also appears at the end of verse 2: "That ye may prove what is that good, and acceptable, and perfect, will of God."

    What does God want out of a believer? He wants acceptable, spiritual worship. And it begins with the presentation of the body as a living sacrifice. Now, it's not just the *physical* body, because then it wouldn't be an act of *spiritual* worship. The body referred to in verse 1 is the whole person, the true self. So because of God's great mercy to us, He calls on us to present ourselves to Him in an act of spiritual worship. Simply put, God saved us so that we might truly and acceptably worship Him.

    b) 1 Peter 2:5

    Chapter 1 contains the wonders of redemptive grace. For example, verse 19 tells of "the precious blood of Christ, as of a lamb without blemish and without spot," verse 18 talks about our new birth, and verses 2-3 of chapter 2 talk about "newborn babes" who "have tasted that the Lord is gracious." Now, as saved individuals, 2:5 describes us, "Ye also, as living stones, are built up a spiritual house, an holy priesthood, to offer up spiritual sacrifices, acceptable to God by Jesus Christ."

    God doesn't live in a house made with hands—in a building made of brick and mortar. He lives in a house made of the living stones of His people. And as holy priests, we are to offer up spiritual sacrifices. Acceptable, true, spiritual worship is offered on the basis of God's transforming work in Christ.

So that's a brief look at the first reason worship is important—Scripture is dominated with it. The second reason worship is important is because:

B. Destiny Is Determined by It

Worship is not an addendum to life, it is at life's core. You see, the people who worship God acceptably enter into eternal life, but the people who do not worship God acceptably enter into eternal death. Worship, then, becomes the core. Time and eternity are determined by the nature of a person's worship.

Now, there are only two kinds of worship that can be offered—acceptable or unacceptable worship. The majority of the world offers unacceptable worship, and God will not accept it. The Bible is explicit on this. There are people today who say that ultimately everybody is going to be saved, but that is not true. The Bible does not say that. But it does say that there are only two kinds of worship—acceptable or unacceptable worship.

1. Unacceptable worship

a) The worship of false gods

People say, "What about all the people who worship their own god because they don't know any better? Surely God will accept them if they're sincere in their worship, won't He?" No! It is unacceptable to God for anyone to worship a non-god, because He is a jealous God and will not tolerate the worship of another (cf. Ex. 34:14; Isa. 48:11b).

The world worships false gods. Look at Romans 1. In verse 21a we read: "When they knew God, they glorified him not as God, neither were thankful." Now frankly, that just means that they wouldn't worship Him or give Him glory, praise, thanks, homage, or adoration. They refused to worship God, which is unacceptable, so He "gave them up to uncleanness" (v. 24), "unto vile affections" (v. 26), and ultimately to their judgment (v. 32). In fact, when they refused to worship God, they began to make images "like corruptible man, and birds, and four-footed beasts, and creeping things" (v. 23). In other words, they turned to idols.

Everybody worships. So when men reject God, they will worship false gods—gods of their own creation. These false gods basically fall into two categories:

(1) Earthly/material gods

An example of an earthly or material god is the god of wealth. This is illustrated in Job 31:24-28: "If I have made gold my hope, or have said to the fine gold, Thou art my confidence; if I rejoiced because my wealth was great, and because mine hand had gotten much; if I beheld the sun when it shined, or the moon walking in brightness; and my heart hath been secretly enticed, or my mouth hath kissed my hand; this also was an iniquity to be punished by the judge; for I should have denied the God who is above." In other words, if I worship what I possess, if I worship my little world, if I go around kissing my own hand, I've denied God. But men do that, and they worship the gods of the material world.

(2) Heavenly/supernatural gods

Deuteronomy 4:14-19a gives us an illustration of this. As the children of Israel were preparing to enter the Promised Land, Moses gave them the following warning: "And the Lord commanded me at that time to teach you statutes and ordinances, that ye might do them in the land which ye go over to possess. Take ye, therefore, good heed unto yourselves; for ye saw no manner of similitude [i.e. form, representation, or image] on the day that the Lord spoke unto you in Horeb out of the midst of the fire; lest ye corrupt yourselves, and make you a carved image, the similitude of any figure, the likeness of male or female, the likeness of any beast that is on the earth, the likeness of any winged fowl that flieth in the air, the likeness of anything that creepeth on the ground, the likeness of any fish that is in the waters beneath the earth; and lest thou lift up thine eyes unto heaven, and when thou seest the sun, and the moon, and the stars, even all the host of heaven, shouldest be driven to worship them, and serve them."

God is never to be reduced to an image—never! Now if you think of God as an old man with a beard, sitting in a big chair—that's bad. Someone once said that idolatry doesn't being with a hammer; it begins with the mind. When someone *conceives* of God in improper terms, he will ultimately cause God to be *made* in improper terms. The idolater who takes his hammer and chisel, and forms a god out of wood, forms the god that's in his mind to begin with. We shouldn't have a visual conception of God whatsoever, because He's never to be reduced to an image. To do so is unacceptable worship.

So, the first kind of unacceptable worship is the worship of false gods. And throughout the Old Testament this is condemned. I want to draw to a conclusion by looking at Isaiah 2:6-10. Here is Isaiah's commentary on what was happening among his people. "Therefore thou hast forsaken thy people, the house of Jacob, because they are filled with customs from the east, and are soothsayers like the Philistines, and they please themselves in the children of foreigners [i.e., they had allowed the foreigners and their foreign gods to invade their

15

thinking and worship]. Their land also is full of silver and gold, neither is there any end of their treasures; their land is also full of horses, neither is there any end of their chariots; their land also is full of idols; they worship the work of their own hands, that which their own fingers have made. And the mean [lit. 'common'] man boweth down, and the great man humbleth himself; therefore, forgive them not. Enter into the rock, and hide in the dust, for fear of the Lord, and for the glory of his majesty."

God's people became idolatrous. They even worshiped the sun (Ezek. 8:16). The pagans worshiped anything they could think of—and the same thing is true today. Every religion that doesn't rightly discern God worships a false god. Every materialist, every irreligious atheist, and every agnostic who wouldn't even darken the door of religion worships some material god of his own invention, even if it's himself. It's all unacceptable to God—it damns the soul.

Focusing on the Facts

1. Why do most people go to church (see p. 8)?
2. What are the music and the sermon in a church service designed to do (see p. 8)?
3. Define the word *worship*. What does the New Testament word for *worship* mean (see p. 8)?
4. What was offered to God in the Old Testament Tabernacle as a symbol of worship (see p. 9)?
5. What act of worship did Mary offer Jesus in John 12:1-3? What attitudes did that act demonstrate (see p. 10)?
6. Explain how the church of today is more like Martha than Mary (Luke 10:38-42; see p. 10).
7. Distinguish between ministry and worship (see p. 10).
8. What is one way Scripture indicates that worship is important (see p. 11)?
9. Summarize the First Commandment in a brief sentence (Ex. 20:2-3; see p. 11).
10. Why did God instruct the Israelites to build the Tabernacle (see p. 11)?
11. Explain how the minimum age requirement for a Levitical priest demonstrates the priority of worship (see p. 12).
12. After having bestowed His mercy on sinful man, what does God require from him, according to Romans 12:1-2 (see p. 13)?
13. What are the only two kinds of worship that can be offered? What kind does the majority of the world offer? What happens to people who do not worship God acceptably (see p. 14)?
14. Will people who worship their own god out of ignorance be accepted by God? Explain (see p. 14).

15. What happens when a person rejects God by refusing to worship Him (Rom. 1:21-26; see p. 14)?

16. Give an example of a material god (see pp. 14-15).

17. What did Moses warn the children of Israel of before they entered the Promised Land, according to Deuteronomy 4:14-19? Why shouldn't we have a visual conception of God (see p. 15)?

18. What does every religion that doesn't rightly discern God do? Does that even include atheists and agnostics (see p. 16)?

Pondering the Principles

1. Do you attend church primarily to worship God? Or do you go to avoid peer pressure, be entertained, or receive some sort of blessing from God? Is your focus on giving to God or getting from Him? Are you so eager to worship God with other Christians that you attend church regularly and you prepare your heart on the way there? Review the definition of *worship* on page 8. Are you worshiping according to the way that word is used in a Christian context? Determine what you should do to improve the attitude of worship you offer to God.

2. Read Luke 10:38-42 and notice the contrast between Martha and Mary. Which woman most closely exemplifies your expression of devotion to Christ? Are you busy with details that do not directly increase your devotion, or are you sitting at the feet of Jesus so that you can get to know Him better? Would you have anointed Christ's feet with a costly ointment in a humble act of worship like Mary did in John 12:1-5? Or would you have criticized such an act as inappropriate? God desires that our worship recognize our humility and His glory, the price of which can never be measured.

3. Meditate on Psalm 95. Why should we worship God? How does the psalm instruct us to worship? What are the consequences of a person hardening his heart and not acknowledging the sovereignty of God? Most people offer unacceptable worship to God. If a neighbor or relative asked why he couldn't worship God in his own way, what would you tell him? Where has God revealed Himself? Pray for an opportunity to share with him the eternal importance of worshiping God in an acceptable manner.

2
True Worship—Part 2

Outline

Introduction

Review
I. The Importance of Worship
   A. Scripture Is Dominated with It
   B. Destiny Is Determined by It
      1. Unacceptable worship
         a) The worship of false gods
            (1) Earthly/material gods
            (2) Heavenly/supernatural gods

Lesson
         b) The worship of the true God in a wrong form
         c) The worship of the true God in a self-styled manner
            (1) Nadab and Abihu (Lev. 10:1-2)
            (2) Saul (1 Sam. 13:18-14a)
            (3) Uzzah (2 Sam. 6:1-9)
            (4) The Pharisees
               (a) Matthew 15:1-9
               (b) Matthew 23:23-28
         d) The worship of the true God with a wrong attitude
            (1) Malachi 1:6-14; 3:13-15; 4:1-6
            (2) Amos 5:21-27
            (3) Hosea 6:4-7
            (4) Isaiah 1:11-20
            (5) Mark 7:6
      2. Acceptable worship
         a) The picture of true worshipers
         b) The production of true worshipers
            (1) Synonymous with salvation
               (a) John 4:23
               (b) Acts 18:7, 13
               (c) Acts 24:14a
            (2) Supported by the gospel record
               (a) Matthew 2:11a
               (b) Matthew 8:1-2

18

Introduction

It's important for us to understand what the Bible teaches about worshiping God. We began our series by briefly looking at John 4:20-24 as the basic text (which we'll examine in more detail later on) and then by moving to a definition of worship. We defined worship as "honor, homage, reverence, adoration, praise, or respect given to God." In John 4:23*b*, our Lord instructs us to "worship the Father in spirit and in truth; for the Father seeketh such to worship him." Worship, then, is giving respect or honor to God. It is to that end that we are called.

Review

In our last lesson we discussed the following:

I. THE IMPORTANCE OF WORSHIP

  A. Scripture Is Dominated with It
  B. Destiny Is Determined by It
    1. Unacceptable worship (see pp. 14-16)
     a) The worship of false gods
      (1) Earthly/material gods
      (2) Heavenly/supernatural gods

Lesson

Now, picking up where we left off last time, let's look at three more kinds of unacceptable worship:

     b) The worship of the true God in a wrong form

       God will not accept the worship of a false god, nor will He accept the worship of the true God if offered in the wrong way. Why? Because the worship of the true God is very specifically established in Scripture, along with the proper mode and manner.

       An illustration of worshiping the true God in a wrong form is found in Exodus 32. Moses was up on Mount Sinai receiving the law from God. And while he was gone, the people, under Aaron's leadership, decided to gather all their gold together, melt it down, fashion it into a golden calf, and worship it. Now, they were not worshiping some other deity; the golden calf was their representation of Jehovah God. They reduced God to an image and were worshiping Him in an unacceptable way.

When Moses returned from Mount Sinai and saw what was going on, he got so angry that he threw down the stone tablets on which the Ten Commandments were written and shattered them (v. 19). Even God's wrath was so great that He threatened to destroy the entire generation (v. 10); but He was gracious (v. 14), and only 3,000 men lost their lives as they were executed on the spot (v. 28).

God will not accept worship that is offered to Him in an unacceptable manner. It's unacceptable to reduce God to an image, a material representation, an idol, or anything that is a result and product of one's own thinking. I often hear people say, "I worship God as I perceive Him to be." Well, if your definition of God doesn't square with the Word of God, your worship is unacceptable—even though you may identify it with the true God.

That leads me to a third kind of unacceptable worship:

c) The worship of the true God in a self-styled manner

Not only is it unacceptable to worship God by reducing Him to an idol or image, but it's also unacceptable to reduce the activity of worship to some personal definition. Let me show you what I mean by giving you a few scriptural illustrations of people who worshiped God in a self-styled way.

(1) Nadab and Abihu (Lev. 10:1-2)

Aaron, the high priest, had two sons, Nadab and Abihu, who were entering the priesthood. Leviticus 10:1 records for us the great day of their ordination into the priesthood. This was the first actual day in which they were to lead the people in the worship of God. But look what happened: "And Nadab and Abihu, the sons of Aaron, took either of them his censer [which, when filled with incense, was symbolic of worship, as its fragrance rose to the nostrils of God], and put fire therein, and put incense thereon, and offered strange fire before the Lord, which he commanded them not. And there went out fire from the Lord, and devoured them, and they died before the Lord."

It's very possible that Nadab and Abihu were drunk, because in verse 9 the Lord gave the following stern warning to Aaron, suggesting to us that his sons were drunk: "Do not drink wine or strong drink, thou, nor thy sons with thee, when ye go into the tabernacle of the congregation, lest ye die."

So, it may well have been that Nadab and Abihu got drunk, went into the Tabernacle, and began to fool around and do things that were not according to God's law for the priest-hood—so God devoured them with fire! God will not accept self-styled, self-invented modes of worship. We are not to worship God on our own terms; we are to worship Him according to the terms prescribed in Scripture.

(2) Saul (1 Sam. 13:8-14a)

King Saul worshiped God in a self-styled manner. In 1 Samuel 13, starting in verse 8 we read, "And he tarried seven days, according to the set time that Samuel had appointed; but Samuel came not to Gilgal, and the people were scattered from him. And Saul said, Bring here a burnt offering to me, and peace offerings. And he offered the burnt offering."

"Now," you say, "is that any big deal?" It sure is! Nobody was allowed to function at the altar except for the priests. Saul wanted to put on a display of power and confidence before the people, so he intruded into the priestly office. Verse 10 continues, "And it came to pass that, as soon as he had ceased offering the burnt offering, behold, Samuel came; and Saul went out to meet him, that he might bless him. And Samuel said, What hast thou done? And Saul said, Because I saw that the people were scattered from me, and that thou camest not within the days appointed, and that the Philistines gathered themselves together at Michmash, therefore, said I, the Philistines will come down now upon me to Gilgal, and I have not made supplication unto the Lord; I forced myself therefore, and offered a burnt offering. And Samuel said to Saul, Thou hast done foolishly: thou hast not kept the commandment of the Lord thy God, which he commanded thee; for now would the Lord have established thy kingdom upon Israel forever. But now thy kingdom shall not continue. The Lord hath sought him a man after his own heart."

God will be worshiped only by someone who is after His own heart. In other words, someone who obeys God's Word. Because of Saul's self-styled worship, there would never again be anyone in Saul's line on the throne.

(3) Uzzah (2 Sam. 6:1-9)

Uzzah was a member of a group known as the Kohathites, who were responsible for transporting the Ark of the Covenant. The Kohathites were raised, from the time they were small, to know nothing but how to transport the ark, and, according to Numbers 4:15, it was never to be touched. The ark had large rings on its sides, through which the Kohathites slid poles and lifted them to their shoulders. This was always how the ark was to be transported—and Uzzah knew that. He was trained from childhood to do it

21

that way, but he took the liberty of putting it on a cart. That was his first mistake, because God will not be handled at the whim of man in a self-styled way—no matter how good the intentions.

So as the ark was being transported on a cart (which was in violation of the rules God had set down), verses 6-7 tell us, "And when they came to Nacon's threshing floor, Uzzah put forth his hand to the ark of God, and took hold of it; for the oxen shook it [i.e., it looked like it was going to fall off the cart]. And the anger of the Lord was kindled against Uzzah; and God smote him there for his error, and there he died by the ark of God."

You see, Uzzah knew better. He had been trained all his life to never touch the ark. But in his own way, he thought he could intrude into God's commandments. The true God cannot be worshiped in a self-styled way!

(4) The Pharisees

The Pharisees tried to worship the true God with their own self-styled system—not according to God's commandments or standards, but according to their own inventions.

(a) Matthew 15:1-9—"Then came to Jesus scribes and Pharisees, who were of Jerusalem, saying, Why do thy disciples transgress the tradition of the elders? For they wash not their hands when they eat bread [i.e., a traditional, ceremonial washing]. But he answered and said unto them, Why do ye also transgress the commandment of God by your tradition?"

You see, they told Jesus that He wasn't worshiping according to their tradition, but Jesus told them that they weren't worshiping according to God's commands. They had invented their own system.

In verses 4-6, Jesus gives them an illustration of how their traditions violated God's commands. Then in verses 7-9, He says, "Ye hypocrites, well did Isaiah prophesy of you, saying, This people draweth near unto me with their mouth, and honoreth me with their lips, but their heart is far from me. But in vain do they worship me, teaching for doctrines the commandments of men."

God isn't interested in all the holy hocus-pocus that goes on in so many "Christian" churches where the traditions of men have been substituted for the commandments of God. God is to be worshiped in spirit and in truth—not through images, rituals, or liturgies.

(b) Matthew 23:23-28—The Lord further indicted the Pharisees in the following passage: "Woe unto you, scribes and Pharisees, hypocrites! For ye pay tithe of mint and anise and cummin, and have omitted the weightier matters of the law, justice, mercy, and faith; these ought ye to have done, and not to leave the other undone. Ye blind guides, who strain at a gnat, and swallow a camel. Woe unto you, scribes and Pharisees, hypocrites! For ye make clean the outside of the cup and of the platter, but within they are full of extortion and excess. . . . For ye are like whited sepulchers, which indeed appear beautiful outward, but are within full of dead men's bones, and of all uncleanness. Even so ye also outwardly appear righteous unto men, but within ye are full of hypocrisy and iniquity."

So, what I'm trying to show you is that there is a category of unacceptable worship. One cannot worship false gods or the true God in a wrong form or in a self-styled manner. It must be according to the prescription of Scripture.

d) The worship of the true God with a wrong attitude

If we eliminate all false gods, all images of the true God, and all self-styled modes of worship, our worship will still be unacceptable if our heart attitude isn't right. This kind of unacceptable worship really hits us where we live. Very few of us worship a false god or an image of the true God. And most of us don't invent our own ways to worship God. We try to worship according to Scripture. But a question each of us needs to ask himself is: Do I have the right attitude? If you don't, it's unacceptable to God!

Let me show you some passages that develop this truth.

(1) Malachi 1:6-14; 3:13-15; 4:1-6

Malachi the prophet indicted the people of God because of their sin. In this marvelous prophecy he pointed out at least seven monumental sins of which they were guilty. But the one that stands out and dominates them all is that they were involved in worshiping God with the wrong attitude. They were just going through the motions, with their hearts far from God.

Let's look at Malachi's indictment. Starting in 1:6, we read, "A son honoreth his father, and a servant his master; if, then, I be a father, where is mine honor? And if I be a master, where is my fear? saith the Lord of hosts unto you, O priests, that despise my name. And ye say, In what way have we despised thy name? Ye offer polluted bread upon mine altar; and ye say, In what way have we polluted thee? In that ye say, The table [or 'altar'] of the Lord is contemptible."

Do you know what they were doing? They were treating their worship with contempt. It was strictly a function, strictly a routine, strictly a ritual. Not only was their heart not involved, but they were actually bringing to God that which was the least rather than that which was the best. But before we pounce on them with both feet, may I remind you that to come to worship with any kind of a wrong attitude—any kind—is to have contempt for worship.

Now, what were they doing? Verse 8 tells us that they were offering the blind for sacrifice. In other words, they would bring blind animals to sacrifice because they were useless to them. A blind animal, since it would have difficulty finding food, would probably die anyway; so they would get rid of it by sacrificing it to God. In addition to that, the blindness might have been caused by disease, so they were offering God diseased animals as well. The worship that they offered to God was to give Him what they couldn't use.

Verse 8 continues: "And if ye offer the lame and sick, is it not evil? Offer it now unto thy governor; will he be pleased with thee, or accept thy person? saith the Lord of hosts. And now, I pray you, beseech God that he will be gracious unto us. This hath been by your means; will he regard your persons? saith the Lord of hosts." In other words, "If this is how you treat God, how do you think He's going to treat you? Do you think He's going to regard you any differently than you regard Him?"

Then he says in verse 10, "Who is there even among you that would shut the doors for nothing? Neither do ye kindle fire on mine altar for nothing. I have no pleasure in you, saith the Lord of hosts, neither will I accept an offering at your hand." There are some things that God won't accept—worship offered in a materialized way, in a self-styled way, and in a half-hearted way.

Verse 11 continues, "For from the rising of the sun even unto the going down of the same, my name shall be great among the nations, and in every place incense shall be offered unto my name, and a pure offering; for my name shall be great among the nations, saith the Lord of hosts." God told them to bring a pure offering. When they were to sacrifice a lamb, it was to be the best lamb in the flock— without spot or blemish. But they weren't doing it!

Look at verses 12-14: "But ye have profaned it, in that ye say, The table of the Lord is polluted; and the fruit of it, even its food, is contemptible. Ye said also, Behold, what a weariness is it! And ye have sniffed at it, saith the Lord of hosts; and ye brought that which was torn, and the lame, and the sick; thus ye brought an offering. Should I accept this of your hand? saith the Lord. But cursed be the

24

deceiver, who hath in his flock a male, and voweth, and sacrificeth unto the Lord a corrupt thing; for I am a great King, saith the Lord of hosts, and my name is terrible among the nations."

Remember, Malachi started out indicting the priests. The priests were the leaders in the sin, but it filtered all the way down to the people. The whole system was rotten from top to bottom. They had contempt for the table of the Lord—and the key is in verse 13, where it says, "Behold, what a weariness." To them the whole exercise of worship was just a big pain in the neck. When it came to worship, they probably said something like, "What a drag! We have to go down there and worship again. Well, let's just get rid of that blind or lame lamb—we don't need it!" They went through the function and the form, but their hearts weren't in it. There was no reality there.

In chapter 3, they went even further. In verses 13-14 they apparently start to bad-mouth God: "Your words have been stout against me, saith the Lord. Yet ye say, What have we spoken so much against thee? Ye have said, It is vain to serve God; and what profit is it that we have kept his ordinance, and that we have walked mournfully before the Lord of hosts?" In other words, they decided that they didn't make enough money serving the Lord—there wasn't enough profit in it.

The results of unacceptable worship are in chapter 4:1, 3: "For, behold, the day cometh, that shall burn like an oven; and all the proud, yea, and all that do wickedly, shall be stubble; and the day that cometh shall burn them up, saith the Lord of hosts, that it shall leave them neither root nor branch. . . . And ye shall tread down the wicked; for they shall be ashes under the soles of your feet in the day that I shall do this, saith the Lord of hosts."

Do you worship with the right attitude?

The previous illustration in Malachi shows that the people of God had come to the place where they were worshiping the true God, in the true way, with the wrong attitude. Their hearts weren't in it. Now look at your own heart. You say, "Well, I don't worship false gods—I worship the true God. I haven't reduced Him to an image, and I haven't invented my own way of worship—like sitting on a mountain contemplating my navel. I'm trying to worship according to God's standards as recorded in His Word." Now, let me ask you some questions: Is your heart in your worship? When it comes time to give, do you give the best of all you have? When it comes time to make your promises to God, do you make Him the promise that is the most reflective of His magnanimity and generosity? Is your heart filled with awe and reverence? If your heart isn't right, your worship is pointless and unacceptable.

(2) Amos 5:21-27

God said, "I hate, I despise your feast days, and I will not take delight in your solemn assemblies [i.e., 'I can't stand your worship']. Though ye offer me burnt offerings and your meal offerings, I will not accept them; neither will I regard the peace offerings of your fat beasts." Now even the good animals are being offered here. They're doing it in the right way, externally, but God will not accept it.

Verse 23 continues, "Take away from me the noise of thy songs; for I will not hear the melody of thine harps. But let justice run down like waters, and righteousness like a mighty stream. Have ye offered unto me sacrifices and offerings in the wilderness forty years, O house of Israel? But ye have borne the tabernacle of your Moloch and Chiun, your images, the star of your god, which ye made to yourselves. Therefore will I cause you to go into captivity beyond Damascus, saith the Lord, whose name is the God of hosts."

In other words, God said, "I'm through with you! On the one hand you come and offer sacrifices to Me, but then you turn right around and worship false gods. You're so engrained, engulfed, and involved in the system of the world, that your worship is hypocritical and unacceptable.

(3) Hosea 6:4-7

"O Ephraim, what shall I do unto thee? O Judah, what shall I do unto thee? For your goodness is like a morning cloud, and like the early dew it goeth away. Therefore have I hewed them by the prophets; I have slain them by the words of my mouth; and thy judgments are as the light that goeth forth. For I desired mercy, and not sacrifice, and the knowledge of God more than burnt offerings. But they, like men, have transgressed the convenant; there have they dealt treacherously against me."

(4) Isaiah 1:11-20

Again God indicts Judah in a similar way to His indictment in Amos, only this time it's through the prophet Isaiah: "To what purpose is the multitude of your sacrifices unto me? saith the Lord; I am full of the burnt offerings of rams, and the fat of fed beasts, and I delight not in the blood of bullocks, or of lambs, or of he-goats." In other words, God said, "I've had it! I'm through!"

Verse 12 continues, "When ye come to appear before me, who hath required this at your hand, to tread my courts? Bring no more vain oblations; incense is an abomination unto me; the new moons and sabbaths, the calling of assemblies, I cannot bear; it is iniquity, even the solemn meeting. Your new moons and your appointed feasts my soul hateth; they are a trouble unto me; I am weary of bearing them. And when ye spread forth your hands, I will hide mine eyes from you; yea, when ye make many prayers, I will not hear. Your hands are full of blood. Wash yourselves, make yourselves clean; put away the evil of your doings from before mine eyes; cease to do evil; learn to do well; seek justice, relieve the oppressed, judge the fatherless, plead for the widow. Come now, and let us reason together, saith the Lord: though your sins be as scarlet, they shall be as white as snow; though they be red like crimson, they shall be as wool. If ye be willing and obedient, ye shall eat the good of the land. But if ye refuse and rebel, ye shall be devoured with the sword; for the mouth of the Lord hath spoken it." And they rebelled and refused the invitation to salvation.

The point is this: Whether it's in Malachi, Amos, Hosea, or Isaiah—the people were doing the right thing, to the right God, in the right way, but with the wrong attitude—and God doesn't accept that!

(5) Mark 7:6

This is similar to Matthew 15 (see pp. 22-23), but I want to look at it since I feel it wraps up this point. "He [Jesus] answered and said unto them [the Pharisees], Well hath Isaiah prophesied of you hypocrites, as it is written, This people honoreth me with their lips, but their heart is far from me." That is unacceptable worship.

If you worship false gods, or if you worship the true God reduced to some kind of image, or if you worship the true God in a self-styled, self-defined way, or if you worship the true God in the right way with the wrong attitude—it's unacceptable and will affect your destiny. God cannot accept one who is unacceptable.

Now, that is the first kind of worship that determines one's destiny. Let me tell you about the second.

2. Acceptable Worship

a) The picture of true worshipers

Psalm 24:3-6 gives a very significant definition of a true, acceptable worshiper: "Who shall ascend into the hill of the Lord? Or who shall stand in His holy place [i.e., 'Who will He accept?']? He who hath clean hands, and a pure heart, who hath not lifted up his soul unto vanity, nor sworn deceitfully. He shall receive the blessing from the Lord, and righteousness from the God of his salvation. This is the generation of them who seek him, who seek thy face."

Those who are acceptable, true worshipers are the ones who have "clean hands" (i.e., they are obedient to God, purified,

27

and made clean), "a pure heart" (i.e., their motives and desires are right), and who truly "seek Him."

b) The production of true worshipers

(1) Synonymous with salvation

Acceptable worship is really a key to understanding the whole matter of salvation. Why? Because *the goal of salvation is to produce acceptable, true worshipers.* If you're truly saved, you're a true, acceptable worshiper. Therefore, as you examine your worship, you're also examining your salvation.

Let me show you some passages to help you understand this.

(a) John 4:23—"But the hour cometh, and now is, when the true worshipers shall worship the Father in spirit and in truth; for the Father seeketh such to worship him." Notice the phrase "true worshipers." That is a term to describe a Christian, a saint, a believer. We could be called *true worshipers* as easily as we could be called Christians, believers, saints, children of God, or any other term which describes our identity and union with Christ.

Also notice, at the end of verse 23, that the Father seeks true worshipers to worship Him. Do you know why the Father sent the Son into the world? Well, in Luke 19:10 Jesus says, "For the Son of man is come to seek and to save that which was lost." Why did God send Christ to seek sinners and save them? We just saw why at the end of verse 23: "For the Father seeketh such to worship Him." *The primary reason we're redeemed is to worship God—not to make us happy.* If He wanted to keep us out of hell, He could have just not created us. But He created man and set out to redeem him, because He seeks to be worshiped. So worshiping God is synonymous with Christian existence—with being a believer.

(b) Acts 18:7, 13—"And he [Paul] departed from there [Athens], and entered into a certain man's house, named Titus Justus, one who worshiped God." The phrase "one who worshiped God" is just another way of saying he was a believer. A believer is one who worships God.

Further, in verse 13, the Jews attack Paul and make the following accusation: "This fellow persuadeth men to worship God." Do you know what Paul was doing in his ministry? He was persuading men to worship God—which is synonymous with salvation. We're not

28

to evangelize men primarily to keep them from hell or to put them in the sphere of God's blessing. Primarily, we're to evangelize men so that they might worship God, showing them that to live apart from worshiping Him is an affront to His holy nature and a rebellious act in His world. *The heart and soul of evangelism is to call men to worship the God who is worthy of worship.*

How tragic it is for the Christian who understands that he is called and redeemed to worship God, to not worship God as fully as he ought.

(c) Acts 24:14a—When Paul discussed with Felix his perspective on life, he said, "But this I confess unto thee that, after the way ['the way' was another term for the Christian faith] which they call heresy, so worship I the God of my fathers." So not only did Paul call people to worship God, he included the fact that he worshiped God as part of his testimony.

(2) Supported by the gospel record

The gospel record supports the fact that people are redeemed for the purpose of worship. In fact, what we find is that when people see the truth of Christ, they have an immediate response of worship—giving honor, homage, respect, reverence, adoration, and praise to God Himself. For example:

(a) Matthew 2:11a—"And when they [the 'wise men' of verse 1] were come into the house, they saw the young child with Mary, his mother, and fell down, and worshiped him." The first thing these king-makers did when they came into His presence was to fall down and worship Him. Why? Because that is the initial response to the reality of Christ.

(b) Matthew 8:1-2—"When he was come down from the mountain, great multitudes followed him. And, behold, there came a leper and worshiped him, saying, Lord, if thou wilt, thou canst make me clean." You see, the leper knew who Jesus was, so he responded in worship.

(c) Matthew 9:18a—"While he spoke these things unto them, behold, there came a certain ruler, and worshiped him."

(d) Matthew 14:33—After the disciples witnessed Jesus walking on the water and stilling a storm, verse 33 tells us, "Then they that were in the boat came and worshiped him, saying, Of a truth, thou art the Son of God."

You see, whoever it is, whenever it is, wherever it is, the instantaneous, spontaneous response to Christ is worship.

(e) Matthew 15:25—"Then came she [a woman of Canaan] and worshiped him, saying, Lord, help me."

(f) Matthew 28:9—"And as they went to tell his disciples, behold, Jesus met them, saying, All hail. And they came and held him by the feet, and worshiped him."

(g) Matthew 28:16-17a—"Then the eleven disciples went away into Galilee, into a mountain where Jesus had appointed them. And when they saw him, they worshiped him."

(h) John 9:31—Jesus healed a man who was born blind. When questioned by the Pharisees about Jesus, he said, "Now we know that God heareth not sinners; but if any man be a worshiper of God, and doeth his will, him he heareth." This man makes an interesting contrast and says that there are only two kinds of people—those God hears, and those He doesn't hear. The people He doesn't hear are sinners, and the people He hears are worshipers. So the contrast is between sinners and worshipers. In fact, the whole world can be divided into "the sinners" and "the worshipers." Therefore, to be saved means to be a worshiper.

(3) Seen in Israel's calling

When God called Israel out as a nation, He called them out for one express purpose—they were called to worship. In fact, the reason for the Tabernacle, the Temple, and the priesthood was to cause the people to focus on worship.

In Deuteronomy 26:5-11 Moses, speaking to the Israelites who were to enter the Promised Land, says, "And thou shalt speak and say before the Lord thy God, A Syrian ready to perish was my father, and he went down into Egypt and sojourned there with a few, and became there a nation, great, mighty, and populous. And the Egyptians badly treated us, and afflicted us, and laid upon us hard bondage; and when we cried unto the Lord God of our fathers, the Lord heard our voice, and looked on our affliction, and our labor, and our oppression. And the Lord brought us forth out of Egypt with a mighty hand, and with an outstretched arm, and with awe-inspiring terror, and with signs, and with wonders; and he hath brought us into this place, and hath given us this land, even a land that floweth with milk and honey."

Now, the Old Testament picture of redemption was deliverance from Egypt. Basically, then, verses 5-9 portray Israel's redemption. Then in verses 10-11 we see the direct response to redemption—worship and rejoicing: "And now, behold, I have brought the first fruits of the land, which thou, O Lord, hast given me. And thou shalt set it before the Lord thy God, and worship before the Lord thy God. And thou shalt rejoice in every good thing which the Lord thy God hath given unto thee, and unto thine house, thou, and the Levite, and the sojourner who is among you." So, worship (v. 10) arose from redemption (vv. 5-9), which resulted in rejoicing (v. 11).

(4) Stated by Paul

In Ephesians 1:3 Paul says, "Blessed be the God and Father of our Lord Jesus Christ, who hath blessed us with all spiritual blessings in heavenly places in Christ." Now, that's a statement of worship, isn't it? And the reason for his statement of worship follows in verses 4-7: "According as he hath chosen us in him before the foundation of the world, that we should be holy and without blame before him, in love having predestinated us unto the adoption of sons by Jesus Christ to himself, according to the good pleasure of his will, to the praise of the glory of his grace, through which he hath made us accepted in the Beloved; in whom we have redemption through his blood, the forgiveness of sins, according to the riches of his grace." You see, worship is the result of redemption.

I submit to you that we're called to worship. Without question, we are called to render acceptable, true, spiritual worship—not just sometimes or once a week—it's to be a way of life.

c) The perspective of true worshipers

We have been saved to worship. Look at Hebrews 12:28: "Wherefore, receiving a kingdom which cannot be moved [i.e., the eternal kingdom], let us have grace, by which we may serve God acceptably with reverence and godly fear." The word "serve" is the Greek verb *latreuō* and should be translated "worship." In Hebrews 10:2, the noun form of *latreuō* is translated "worshipers." Basically, then, the idea of verse 28 is as follows: "Since we have received the kingdom which cannot be moved, and since we have become worshipers of God, then let us have the graciousness to respond to God who has made us worshipers, by worshiping God acceptably." Put in Pauline terms, it comes out like this: "Present your bodies a living sacrifice, holy, acceptable unto God, which is your reasonable service [lit., 'spiritual worship']" (Rom. 12:1).

31

Going back to Hebrews 12, notice verses 28b-29: "By which we may serve [lit., 'worship'] God acceptably with reverence and godly fear; for our God is a consuming fire." In other words, we'd better worship God acceptably—or else! Acceptable worship, first of all, is the result of salvation. But filling out that worship and living up to its fullness comes as a result of the graciousness of the believer who willingly offers his body in an act of spiritual service—worshiping God acceptably with reverence and godly fear. And because God is a consuming fire, we need to be worried about the consequence if we don't worship Him properly!

By way of application, if you have trouble and problems in your life, and you're going through a checklist to determine why these things may be occurring, put at the top of that checklist: "Perhaps I'm not worshiping God with a true heart and a true spirit and don't have the grace to worship God acceptably with reverence and godly fear." If so, the consequences may be His chastening.

Focusing on the Facts

1. Besides worshiping false gods, what other kinds of unacceptable worship are there (see pp. 19-20, 23)?
2. How did the Israelites worship the true God in an unacceptable manner? What were the consequences of that misdirected worship (see pp. 19-20)?
3. What happened to Nadab and Abihu, who failed to worship God in the proper manner (see p. 20)?
4. Although Saul had good intentions, was his priestly display acceptable to God? Why? As a result, what type of person did the Lord seek to lead His people (1 Sam. 13:14; see p. 21)?
5. What should Uzzah have known not to do as he was transporting the ark (see pp. 21-22)?
6. Why did Jesus condemn the way the Pharisees were worshiping God (Matt. 15:1-9; see p. 22)?
7. How did the Pharisees appear outwardly? What really characterized their lives (Matt. 23:28; p. 22)?
8. For what primary sin did Malachi indict the people of Israel? How was that expressed (see pp. 23-24)?
9. What are the results of worshiping God with the wrong attitude, according to Malachi 4:1 and 3 (see p. 25)?
10. Why did God not take delight in the worship of Israel, according to Amos 5:21-27 (see p. 26)?
11. According to Psalm 24:3-5, who is the one whose worship is acceptable to God? What are two things such a person receives from God (see pp. 26-27)?
12. What is the goal of salvation? Support your answer with Scripture (see p. 28).

13. What is the primary reason for evangelizing? What would be some secondary reasons (see pp. 28-29)?

14. When did people worship Jesus in the gospels (see pp. 29-30)?

15. What two categories of people did the blind man of John 9 correctly recognize (v. 31; see p. 30)?

16. What function did the Tabernacle, the Temple, and the priesthood play in the nation of Israel (see p. 30)?

17. Identify the Old Testament picture of redemption. What are the two responses to redemption, according to Deuteronomy 26:10-11 (see p. 31)?

18. How often are we called to render acceptable worship to God (see p. 31)?

19. Why should man be worried about the consequence of not worshiping God properly (Heb. 12:28-29; see p. 32)?

Pondering the Principles

1. We live in a permissive society that condones all kinds of self-expression—however bizarre. We are careful to not infringe on anyone's personal rights as they adamantly request, "Let me do things my way. I've got to be me. I'm not hurting anybody." We hesitate to burst the bubble of someone who has a self-deluded perspective of reality. But it may be necessary to open such a person's eyes. When you share the truth of the Bible with someone like that, prepare yourself with prayer that the Spirit would guide your thoughts and words and that He would soften the person's heart. If you know of any published materials that can acquaint you with his religious world view, become familiar with them. Don't be afraid to shine light into his darkness just because you don't fully comprehend his religious beliefs, since your primary objective is to present the gospel.

2. Since you are reading this book, you probably aren't worshiping false gods or even the true God in the wrong way or in a self-styled manner. However, you may be worshiping God with the wrong attitude. Are you worshiping Him because He has created you and saved you from sin and death? Do you go through the same routine Sunday after Sunday without really considering what God has done for you? Are you using church attendance solely as a means of blessing or acceptance by God? If so, begin this very day to praise God for who He is and what He has done. Then, as you worship next Sunday in church, make a point of concentrating on the hymns that are sung, the Scripture that is read, and the message that is preached, that your heart might offer gratitude to God as you depart to serve Him with your life. Meditate on Psalm 86, noting the psalmist's requests and his reasons for worshiping God.

3
True Worship—Part 3

Outline

Introduction

Review
I. The Importance of Worship
   A. Scripture Is Dominated with It
   B. Destiny Is Determined by It
     1. Unacceptable worship
     2. Acceptable worship
       a) The picture of true worshipers
       b) The production of true worshipers
       c) The perspective of true worshipers

Lesson
       d) The personal characteristics of true worshipers
        (1) Our treatment of fellow believers
        (2) Winning someone to Jesus Christ
        (3) Giving money to meet needs
        (4) Living a life of goodness, righteousness, and truth
        (5) Being filled with the fruits of righteousness
        (6) Living a life of godliness and honesty
        (7) Praising God and giving Him thanks
       e) The purpose for the assembly of true worshipers
   C. Eternity and Redemptive History Are Described by It
     1. Pre-creation history
     2. Pre-Fall history
     3. Post-Fall history
       a) Cain and Abel
       b) The patriarchs
       c) The nation Israel
        (1) In the desert
        (2) In the Promised Land
       d) Jesus
     4. Present history
     5. Future history
       a) Revelation 4:10-11*a*
       b) Revelation 5:14

     c) Revelation 11:15*b*-17*a*
     d) Revelation 14:6-7
     e) Revelation 15:4*a*
     f) Revelation 19:4
     g) Revelation 19:10*a*
     h) Revelation 22:8-9
  D. Christ Commanded It

Introduction

Someone once said, "Worship is to Christian living what the mainspring is to a watch." To worship God is the very core of a Christian's response to God—the very heart of his activity. You say, "What does it mean to worship?" It's simply to recognize the worth, value, majesty, honor, and glory of God. The chief duty of every believer is to see the worth of God and to give Him the honor and glory that is due His name.

Review

Thus far in our study of worship we have looked at:

I. THE IMPORTANCE OF WORSHIP

  A. Scripture Is Dominated with It (see pp. 11-14)

  B. Destiny Is Determined by It
     1. Unacceptable worship

Now, there are many examples I could use to illustrate unacceptable worship, but I chose the following one because of its relevance to today.

Masonry: fraternal order or false religion?

In 1717 a group that is now known as the Masonic Lodge, or the Masons, was formed. Although they do not wish to be known as a religion, they are, by definition, clearly a religion—and a classic illustration of unacceptable worship.

The *Iowa Quarterly Bulletin* of April 1917 (p. 54), a Masonic publication, says this: "Masonry is a Divinely appointed institution, designed to draw men nearer to God, to give them a clearer conception of their proper relationship to God as their Heavenly Father, to men as their brethren and the ultimate destiny of the human soul." Now that's obviously a religion—even though they don't want to admit it!

Albert Pike, who has been called by fellow Masons "one of the most distinguished Masons the Western World has produced," says in *Morals and Dogmas*, page 23 (this is also found in *Hertel's Bible*, page 9, which is the Mason's edition of the Bible): "It [Masonry] reverences all the great reformers. It sees in Moses, the Lawgiver of the Jews, in Confucius and Zoroaster, in Jesus of Nazareth, and in the Arabian Iconoclast, Great Teachers of Morality, and Eminent Reformers, if no more; And allows every brother of the Order to assign to each such higher and even Divine Character as his Creed and Truth require. . . .

We do not undervalue the importance of any Truth. We utter no word that can be deemed irreverent by anyone of any faith. We do not tell the Moslem that it is only important for him to believe that there is but one God, and wholly unessential whether Mahomet was His prophet. We do not tell the Hebrew that the Messiah whom he expects was born in Bethlehem nearly two thousand years ago; and that he is a heretic because he will not so believe. And as little do we tell the sincere Christian that Jesus of Nazareth was but a man like us, or His history but the unreal revival of an older legend. To do either is beyond our jurisdiction. Masonry, of no one age, belongs to all time; of no one religion, it finds its great truths in all. To every Mason, there is a God; One Supreme, Infinite in Goodness, Wisdom, Foresight, Justice, and Benevolence; Creator, Disposer, and Preserver of all things. How, or by what intermediates He creates and acts, and in what way He unfolds and manifests Himself, Masonry leaves to creeds and religions to inquire." In other words, they say they believe in God, but *you* can decide who He is, what He wants, and how to get to Him.

When a person become a Mason, he's not allowed to speak certain secret words. If you have ever known a Mason, you are probably aware of the fact that he would never reveal any of those secret words. However, I would like to reveal them: The most sacred word, assumed to be the word for God, is transmitted to the candidate as he is "raised" into the Master Mason Degree, as he assumes the position of the "five points of fellowship" (toe to toe, knee to knee, chest to chest, cheek to cheek, and mouth to ear). Whispered into his ear is the word *Mah-Ha-Bone.* This "sacred" word, the candidate is told, must never be spoken aloud, never revealed, and always concealed.

The Mason in the Royal Arch Degree (York Rite), a degree through which the Knight Templar is to pass on his way to the supposed "Christian Degree," has another secret name revealed to him at his initiation ceremony. The name of the True God, "rediscovered," is "Jah-Bul-On." This is the Royal Arch Masons' "Trinity." "Jah" is an abbreviation for the Hebrew name for God: Jahweh, Jehovah. "Bul" is the name for the Assyrian deity and is mentioned throughout the Old Testament as "Baal." "On" is the Egyptian sun god.

Pike, in *Morals and Dogmas* (p. 854) says, "To achieve it [salvation] the Mason must first attain a solid conviction, founded upon reason, that he hath within him a spiritual nature, a soul that is not to die when the body is dissolved, but is to continue to exist and to advance toward perfection through all ages of eternity, and to see more and more clearly, as it draws nearer unto God the light of the Divine Presence." Frankly, that's a bunch of hocus-pocus that means nothing.

In the Mason's Bible (p. 34) it says, "In the opening of the lodge, the Great Architect of the Universe must be worshiped, and his blessings upon the work about to be done must be supplicated; at the same time, prayer should be offered for peace and harmony in the closing of the lodge." This non-descriptive "Great Architect" *must* be worshiped. Who is he? Any god you design.

Pike also claims that at Masonic altars, "the Christian, the Hebrew, the Moslem, the Brahmin, the followers of Confucius and Zoroaster, can assemble as brethren and unite in prayer to the one God."

In *Short Talk Bulletin* (Vol. 36, No. 8, p. 7) it says, "The chaplain of the masonic lodge who prays as the voice of the lodge does not pray in the name of the Carpenter of Nazareth or the name of Jehovah or the name of Allah. He prays to the Grand Artificer or the Great Architect of the Universe. Under that title men of all faiths may find each his own deity. Failure to mention any deity by name is not denial, but merely the practice of a gracious courtesy, so that each man for whom prayer is offered can hear the name of his own deity in the all inclusive title of Great Architect."

Well, I think you get the point. *Masonry is a satanic false religion.* It says, "Yes, we believe in the true God," but reduces Him to a wrong form, and worships Him in a wrong manner, with a wrong heart attitude. It's unacceptable; unfortunately there are myriad such unacceptable kinds of worship. Those who practice them may think they're worshiping God—but they're not!

2. Acceptable worship

Acceptable worship determines our destiny and distinguishes us as believers. In fact, the goal of salvation is to create true worshipers.

a) The picture of true worshipers (see pp. 27-28)

Psalm 24:3-6 is perhaps the loveliest Old Testament picture of a true worshiper. It says, "Who shall ascend into the hill of the Lord? Or who shall stand in his holy place? He who hath clean hands, and a pure heart, who hath not lifted up his soul unto vanity, nor sworn deceitfully. He shall receive the blessing from the Lord, and righteousness from the God of his salvation. This is the generation of them who seek him, who seek thy face." True worshipers are the pure, the righteous, and the holy.

b) The production of true worshipers (see pp. 28-31)

In our last lesson we saw that the primary purpose of redemption is to create true worshipers who worship God acceptably.

c) The perspective of true worshipers (see pp. 31-32)

Picking up where we left off, we ended the last lesson looking at Hebrews 12:28-29. The writer of Hebrews says, "Wherefore, receiving a kingdom which cannot be moved, let us have grace, by which we may serve [Gk., *latreuō*, 'worship'] God acceptably with reverence and godly fear; for our God is a consuming fire." When we worship God acceptably, there is to be a balance between reverence and fear. Reverence can be looked at as positive—affirming the value and worth of God. Fear can be looked at as negative—affirming the judging, chastening, punishing, "consuming fire" of verse 29. So, a true worshiper worships out of reverence for God, as well as fear of Him.

If we have been redeemed, we are the true worshipers. And as true worshipers, we must worship acceptably. Now, I admit that even though we are true worshipers, we don't always worship as truly as we ought because of the sin that is in us; but that is our goal. We are called to worship God acceptably with the positive affirmation that because He is a consuming fire, we have reason to fear if we don't worship Him acceptably.

Lesson

d) The personal characteristics of true worshipers

How do we manifest true acceptable worship in our everyday lives?

(1) Our treatment of fellow believers

Romans 14 talks about not making a weaker brother stumble or destroying him with the liberty we may have. Then in verse 18*a* Paul says, "For he that in these things serveth Christ is acceptable to God." In other words, acceptable worship is a matter of how we treat our fellow believers.

(2) Winning someone to Jesus Christ

In Romans 15:16, Paul, thanking God for the grace that called him into the ministry, makes an amazing statement: "That I should be the minister of Jesus Christ to the Gentiles, ministering the gospel of God, that the offering up of the Gentiles might be acceptable." In other words, Paul saw his Gentile converts as acceptable offerings that were given to God. So winning someone to Jesus Christ is acceptable worship. The gaining of a soul can be offered to God as an act of holy, acceptable worship.

(3) Giving money to meet needs

Paul wrote to the Philippians, in part, to thank them for a gift of money they had sent him. He was glad they sent it because it was an act of love. In 4:18 he says, "But I have all, and abound. I am full, having received of Epaphroditus the things which were sent from you, an odor of a sweet smell, a sacrifice acceptable, well pleasing to God." Their gift of money to meet Paul's need was an acceptable sacrifice to God. Acceptable worship is giving your resources to support the saints, the work of the church, and the ministry of Christ.

Now the sum of these first three characteristics of acceptable worship—how we treat fellow Christians, winning non-Christians to Christ, and giving money to meet needs—is sharing. *Worship is sharing*—sharing your love, sharing the gospel, and sharing your resources. That exalts, honors, and glorifies God because it puts Him on display through your life and shows that you're obedient to Him. It also shows that you love those whom He loves—the saints, the lost, and the needy. Sharing is acceptable worship.

(4) Living a life of goodness, righteousness, and truth

In Ephesians 5:8b-10 Paul says, "Walk as children of light (for the fruit of the Spirit [lit., 'light'] is in all goodness and righteousness and truth), proving what is acceptable unto the Lord." Living a life of goodness, righteousness, and truth (i.e., personal holiness) is a life of acceptable worship.

(5) Being filled with the fruits of righteousness

In Philippians 1:11 Paul prays that the Philippians might be "Filled with the fruits of righteousness, which are by Jesus Christ, unto the glory and praise of God." So again we see that righteousness, holiness, goodness, and godliness is acceptable worship.

(6) Living a life of godliness and honesty

In 1 Timothy 2:3 Paul says, "For this is good and acceptable in the sight of God, our Savior." You say, "What is good and acceptable?" Look at the end of verse 2: "A quiet and peaceable life in all godliness and honesty." Godliness and honesty, along with righteousness, goodness, truth, and holiness, are characteristics of acceptable worship.

Now, I gave you three scriptures that present worship as sharing with others, and three scriptures that relate worship to personal holiness. So worship is a way of life that manifests itself in personal righteousness and extends to loving the brethren, proclaiming to the lost, and freeing resources to meet needs. Finally, acceptable worship is seen as:

(7) Praising God and giving Him thanks

Hebrews 13:15 says, "By him [Jesus Christ], therefore, let us offer the sacrifice of praise to God continually, that is, the fruit of our lips giving thanks to his name." This is really the climax, isn't it? When we come together to worship, we sing, we praise God with our hearts and our lips, and we say thanks.

Now look at verse 16: "But to do good and to share forget not; for with such sacrifices God is well pleased." Did you get that? God wants us to come together to praise and glorify His name and to say thanks to Him. But He doesn't want us to forget that our worship is a way of life—doing good and sharing with others. You see? Hebrews 13:15-16 really sums up a worshiping life.

Worship is for every day—not just Sundays

If you think that you can live any way you want on Monday through Saturday and then go to church on Sunday and worship, you're dead wrong! Worship doesn't occur in a vacuum, nor is it stimulated by artificial gimmickry. If you have to be in a church building or hear a certain kind of mood music to worship, what you're doing *isn't* worship. You should be able to worship God on the freeway during rush hour. But to do so, your heart must be right. You see, when we come together in the assembly of the saints to worship God, if it isn't an extension of a worshiping life, true worship won't occur. That is why Hebrews 13:15-16 tells us to assemble collectively to "Offer the sacrifice of praise to God continually, that is, the fruit of our lips giving thanks to his name." But we can't forget *"to do good and to share"* as a way of life, or we'll never generate any worship on Sunday. Worship must be a way of life!

e) The purpose for the assembly of true worshipers

Even though our worship is to be a way of life, we also need to be involved in the corporate worship that occurs once a week. Why? Because our worship on Sunday stimulates us to worship during the rest of the week. Hebrews 10 says, "Let us draw near with a true heart. . . . Not forsaking the assembling of ourselves together" (vv. 22*a*, 25*a*). Why? Because verse 24 tells us that we are to come together to stimulate one another "unto love and to good works." We have to be living a life of sharing and righteousness out in the world in order to worship. And we are stimulated to do those things as we assemble ourselves together for the purpose of worship. One feeds the other. We must be in the fellowship of the saints, in the congregation of the righteous, among the people in whom God dwells—because it is there that we are stimulated to love and good works. As that stimulation affects our soul, we go out "to do good and to share" (Heb. 13:16*a*). Then, when we come back into the assembly, we overflow in praise with a continual heart of worshipful thanksgiving.

Now, if you're not in this worshiping "cycle," you'd better get in. How? Confess your sins and start right now. People say, "Well, I've got so many problems in my Christian life, I just can't be committed to being consistent." People who say that basically have one of two problems: either they're not worshiping six days a week with a worshiping life, or they're not worshiping one day a week in the assembly of the saints. We need both! If you go to church just when it's convenient, you're never going to get your act together. You can't do it on your own—you've got to have the faithful, consistent stimulation to love and good works that a body of people brings to bear on your life. Unfortunately, we live in such an easy-come-easy-go, casual, flippant society, that people don't make those kinds of consistent, faithful commitments—and then they wonder why they can't get their act together! We all need to join with a worshiping assembly as well as live each day with a worshiping life.

Worship is important because Scripture is dominated with it, destiny is determined by it, and third:

C. Eternity and Redemptive History Are Described by It

Worship is important because it's the major theme of eternity and redemptive history.

1. Pre-creation history

In eternity past, before men were created, what existed? The Trinity and the angels. What did they do? Well, Nehemiah 9:6b says, "And the host of heaven worshipeth thee." What went on in eternity past? Worship (cf. Job 38:4-7).

2. Pre-Fall history

When Adam and Eve were created, they worshiped God as they walked and talked with Him in the Garden. However, sin entered the picture when Eve chose to worship Satan, and Adam chose to worship Eve. As soon as they ceased worshiping God, they fell (Gen. 3:1-13).

3. Post-Fall history

a) Cain and Abel

In Genesis 4, the first division among men came between Cain and Abel over the way they worshiped. Abel brought an acceptable offering (4:4), but Cain's was unacceptable (4:5).

b) The patriarchs

When the patriarchs worshiped God properly, they were blessed, but when they worshiped Him unacceptably they were chastened.

c) The nation Israel

(1) In the desert

When the nation of Israel was taken out of Egypt, they wandered for forty years in the Sinai desert until an entire generation died. They lost their lives without entering the Promised Land simply because they failed to worship God properly (Num. 14:22-23). Even Moses never entered the land, because he failed to worship God properly (Num. 20:7-12).

(2) In the Promised Land

When the nation of Israel finally got into the land, they

worshiped God as He wanted to be worshiped and were subsequently blessed (Neh. 9:3, 1 Chron. 29:20-25). However, the time came when they did not worship God properly (Acts 7:42-43), so He punished them and ultimately scattered them all over the world.

d) Jesus

When Jesus began His ministry, He went to Jerusalem, walked into the place of worship, took a whip, and cleaned the place out (John 2:13-17). After He dealt with the corrupt worshipers in John 2, He called for true worshipers in John 4:23-24. Worship was always the issue—the central theme of redemptive history.

4. Present history

When the church was born, it was an assembly of worshipers. Philippians 3:3 is one of the greatest statements on worship in the Bible—a definition of the church: "For we are the circumcision, which worship God in the spirit, and rejoice in Christ Jesus, and have no confidence in the flesh." In other words, the church is uniquely identified as God's people—but not through physical circumcision. The church is made up of those who worship God in their spirit, rejoicing in Christ, with no confidence in the flesh.

5. Future history

When history consummates in the glory of the return of Christ, it will consummate in worship. Worship is the theme of heaven and of eternity. For example:

a) Revelation 4:10-11*a*—"The four and twenty elders fall down before him that is seated on the throne, and worship him that liveth forever and ever, and cast their crowns before the throne, saying, Thou art worthy, O Lord, to receive glory and honor and power."

b) Revelation 5:14—"And the four living creatures said, Amen. And the four and twenty elders fell down, and worshiped him that liveth forever and ever."

c) Revelation 11:15*b*-17*a*—"And there were great voices in heaven, saying, The kingdom of this world is become the kingdom of our Lord, and of his Christ; and he shall reign forever and ever. And the four and twenty elders, who sat before God on their thrones, fell upon their faces, and worshiped God, saying, We give thee thanks, O Lord God Almighty."

d) Revelation 14:6-7—"And I saw another angel fly in the midst of heaven, having the everlasting gospel to preach unto them that dwell on the earth, and to every nation, and kindred, and tongue, and people, saying with a loud voice, Fear God, and give glory to him; for the hour of his judgment is come; and worship him that made heaven, and earth, and the sea, and the fountains of waters." Notice that the message of the everlasting gospel is to worship God!

e) Revelation 15:4a—"Who shall not fear thee, O Lord, and glorify thy name? For thou only art holy; for all nations shall come and worship before thee."

f) Revelation 19:4—"And the four and twenty elders and the four living creatures fell down and worshiped God that sat on the throne, saying, Amen. Hallelujah!"

g) Revelation 19:10a—"And I [John] fell at his [the angel's] feet to worship him. And he said unto me, See thou do it not! I am thy fellow servant, and of thy brethren that have the testimony of Jesus. Worship God."

h) Revelation 22:8-9—"And I, John, saw these things, and heard them. And when I had heard and seen, I fell down to worship before the feet of the angel who showed me these things. Then saith he unto me, See thou do it not; for I am thy fellow servant, and of thy brethren, the prophets, and of them who keep the words of this book. Worship God."

That's the theme of eternity and redemptive history: to worship the true, living, and glorious God.

So, Scripture calls us to worship, destiny calls us to worship, and just in case somebody might fall through the cracks and think they don't need to worship, the fourth reason it's important to worship is because:

D. Christ Commanded It

In Matthew 4:10b our Lord says, "For it is written, Thou shalt worship the Lord, thy God, and him only shalt thou serve." This statement was made directly to Satan, but it applies to every being ever created. All are responsible to worship God.

Do you worship God as a way of life? You should! If you find it difficult to worship the Lord when you attend church on Sundays, it isn't because the music isn't right, or because the atmosphere isn't right, or because you get distracted. If you can't worship, it's because you're not worshiping during the rest of the week. Worship can't just happen once a week—it's a way of life. And when Christians do come together once a week, there should be a bursting out of true praise and worship of the heart. The worship that is enjoyed individually will be enriched and enhanced when brought into the joy of the assembly. Worship then becomes all the more glorious!

Focusing on the Facts

1. What are we to recognize when we worship (see p. 35)?
2. Give a brief description of what the Masonic Lodge believes about worship-

ing God and how it relates to other religions (see pp. 35-37).

3. What is the twofold perspective of true worshipers, according to Hebrews 12:28-29 (see pp. 37-38)?

4. Match the ways we can manifest acceptable worship in our daily lives with the appropriate verses (see pp. 38-39).

   a. Treating fellow believers   a. Hebrews 13:15
   b. Leading someone to Christ   b. Romans 14:18
   c. Giving money for needs   c. Philippians 4:18
   d. Living a righteous life   d. Ephesians 5:8-10
   e. Living a peaceable life   e. Romans 15:16
   f. Giving God thanks   f. 1 Timothy 2:3

5. What three things that glorify God does a worshiper share? Explain how that is done (see p. 39).

6. Describe the quality of life that a worshiper is to live (Phil. 1:11; see pp. 39-40).

7. Summarize the two aspects of worship, as indicated in Hebrews 13:15-16 (see pp. 39-40).

8. Where should you be able to worship God? What should be the extension of a worshiping life (see p. 40)?

9. Why do Christians need to be involved in corporate worship once a week (Heb. 10:22, 24-25; see p. 41)?

10. Whom did Adam and Eve choose to worship rather than God (see p. 41)?

11. Over what was the first division among men (see p. 41)?

12. What were the consequences of Israel failing to worship properly in the desert (Num. 14:22-23; see p. 41)?

13. According to Philippians 3:3, what type of people is the church made up of (see p. 42)?

14. What is the theme of heaven and eternity? Cite some scriptures to support your answer (see pp. 42-43).

15. What mistake did the Apostle John make in Revelation 19:10 and 22:8-9? What was he instructed to do instead (see p. 43)?

16. What is the fourth reason that worship is important (Matt. 4:10; see p. 43)?

Pondering the Principles

1. Review the personal characteristics of true worshipers discussed on pages 38-39. Are you fulfilling the duty of worshiping properly in each of those areas? In which area are you the weakest? As you yield yourself to the control of the Holy Spirit, prayerfully consider how you will strengthen that area this week.

2. The writer of Hebrews exhorted his readers, "And let us consider how to stimulate one another to love and good deeds, not forsaking our own assembling together, as is the habit of some, but encouraging one another;

and all the more, as you see the day drawing near" (Heb. 10:24-25; NASB*). Do you actually take time to consider how to stimulate other Christians? How can you stimulate your peers without appearing to be a self-acclaimed authority? What suggestion does 1 Peter 5:2-3 offer? Why do you think it's still necessary to assemble together? Could Christians in this modern age merely watch church services on T.V. and communicate with other believers by phone? If you lack commitment and accountability to a local body of believers, plan to become a member of a church near you that teaches the Word of God.

*New American Standard Bible.

4
True Worship—Part 4

Outline

Introduction

Review
I. The Importance of Worship
   A. Scripture Is Dominated with It
   B. Destiny Is Determined by It
   C. Eternity and Redemptive History Are Described by It
   D. Christ Commanded It

Lesson
II. The Source (Basis) of Worship
   A. The Response to Christ's Death (Ps. 22:22-27)
   B. The Reason for Israel's Sacrifices (Ex. 20:22-26)
   C. The Revelation of Isaiah's Prophecy (Isa. 66:22-23)
   D. The Reaction of a Converted Sinner (1 Cor. 14:23-25)

III. The Object of Worship
   A. God as Spirit (His Essential Nature)
      1. The spirituality of God
         a) He cannot be reduced to an image
         b) He cannot be confined to a place
            (1) Mt. Gerizim/Jerusalem
            (2) The Tabernacle/Temple

Introduction

There's nothing more important in a person's life than to be oriented toward worshiping God. To worship God is the supreme activity of the universe. Now, we've been involved in a very essential study of acceptable, true, spiritual worship. Our central text has been John 4:20-24, but we have been examining many other passages on this subject. First of all, at the end of John 4:23, we find that "the Father seeketh such [true worshipers] to worship Him."

Review

I. THE IMPORTANCE OF WORSHIP

A. Scripture Is Dominated with It (see pp. 11-14)

B. Destiny Is Determined by It (see pp. 35-41)

C. Eternity and Redemptive History Are Described by It (see pp. 41-43)

D. Christ Commanded It (see p. 43)

Lesson

Now let's look at:

II. THE SOURCE (BASIS) OF WORSHIP

The goal of salvation is worship. The reason God redeems people is so that they may be worshipers. In 2 Corinthians 4:15 Paul says, "For all things are for your sakes, that the abundant grace might through the thanksgiving of many redound to the glory of God." In other words, Paul said, "Everything we do, we do that you might receive the grace of God; and then in response, give thanks and glory to God." Everything is ultimately geared to produce worship.

Now, acceptable worship is the direct result of Christ's saving work. In Luke 19:10 the Lord says that He came into the world "to seek and to save that which was lost." If you connect this verse with John 4:23b, which tells us that the Father seeks true worshipers, you get the whole picture of Christ's coming. The worshipers that God seeks become worshipers through salvation in Christ. So the source, or basis, of worship is salvation. Let's look at a few passages which support this truth.

A. The Response to Christ's Death (Ps. 22:22-27)

Psalm 22:1-21 is an explicit prophetic picture of the crucifixion of Christ. Many of the things that were said in this passage were directly fulfilled on the cross. For example: verse 1 (Matt. 27:46); verses 6-8, 12-13 (Matt. 27:22-25, 39-44); verse 14 (Matt. 27:35a; John 19:34b); verse 15 (John 19:28); verse 16b (John 20:25); verses 16a, 17b (Luke 23:35); verse 18 (John 19:23-24). It was predicted that Christ would go to the cross and suffer those things—but for what? The answer to that begins in verse 22: "I will declare thy name unto my brethren; in the midst of the congregation will I praise thee. Ye who fear the Lord, praise him; all ye, the seed of Jacob, glorify him; and fear him, all ye, the seed of Israel. For he hath not despised nor abhorred the affliction of the afflicted, neither hath he hidden his face from him; but when he cried unto him, he heard." The immediate response to the work of Christ is praise, isn't it?

Verse 25 continues, "My praise shall be of thee in the great congregation; I will pay my vows before them that fear him. The meek shall eat and be satisfied; they shall praise the Lord that seek him; your heart shall live forever [i.e., the everlasting life that comes through the death of Christ]. All the ends of the world shall remember and turn unto the Lord; and all the kindreds of the nations shall worship before thee."

47

Psalm 22, then, is a rather explicit indication that the goal of redemption is worship. The truth that salvation is the basis of worship is also illustrated by:

B. The Reason for Israel's Sacrifices (Ex. 20:22-26)

Look at Exodus 19:7-8: "And Moses came and called for the elders of the people, and laid before their faces all these words which the Lord commanded him. And all the people answered together, and said, All that the Lord hath spoken we will do. And Moses returned the words of the people unto the Lord."

This is the greatest illustration of wishful thinking in all of history. It was a nice thought, but God didn't believe it for one minute. God knew they would never be able to approach Him on the basis of their lawkeeping or their self-righteousness. So after He gives them the specifics of the Ten Commandments in 20:1-17, He gives them a gracious provision in verses 22-26: "And the Lord said unto Moses, Thus thou shalt say unto the children of Israel, Ye have seen that I have talked with you from heaven. Ye shall not make with me gods of silver, neither shall ye make unto you gods of gold. An altar of earth thou shalt make unto me, and shalt sacrifice thereon thy burnt offerings, and thy peace offerings, thy sheep, and thine oxen; in all places where I record my name I will come unto thee, and I will bless thee. And if thou wilt make me an altar of stone thou shalt not build it of hewn stone; for if thou lift up thy tool upon it, thou hast polluted it. Neither shalt thou go up by steps unto mine altar, that thy nakedness be not exposed thereon."

You say, "What's the point?" Well, God knew that men had no right and no access on their own to worship Him, because they could not keep His law—no matter what they *thought* they could do. So God established an altar, and the sacrifices that were placed upon it, as the basis of worship. Sacrifice made communion possible.

The death of Christ,then was to provide God with the basis for seeking after true worshipers. As we meet at the cross, our sin is dealt with, we are purified by the blood of Jesus Christ, and we become acceptable worshipers of the Father. So our salvation, which is made possible by the sacrificial death of Christ, is the source of our worship.

C. The Revelation of Isaiah's Prophecy (Isa. 66:22-23)

The book of Isaiah sweeps through redemptive history in a marvelous way. The first portion of the book (chapters 1-39) talks about God's judgment, and then it moves into the great future—the coming of the Messiah and the coming of the kingdom. Then, in 66:22-23, it goes beyond the millennial kingdom into the eternal state and says, "For as the new heavens and the new earth, which I will make, shall remain before me, saith the Lord, so shall your seed and your name remain. And it shall come to pass that, from one new moon to another, and from one sabbath to another, shall all flesh come to worship before me, saith the Lord."

In chapters 52 and 53, Isaiah talks about the suffering Messiah who was to die on the cross to pay the price for sin. And then in chapter 66 it tells us why—so that He might produce a generation of eternal worshipers who worship the true and living God.

D. The Reaction of a Converted Sinner (1 Cor. 14:23-25)

In 1 Corinthians 14:23-25 Paul says, "If, therefore, the whole church be come together into one place, and all speak with tongues, and there come in those that are unlearned, or unbelievers, will they not say that ye are mad [or insane]? But if all prophesy [i.e., speak the truth of God in an understood language], and there come in one that believeth not, or one unlearned, he is convicted of all, he is judged of all. And thus are the secrets of his heart made manifest."

Now, if you want to really crack open somebody's heart, don't speak in tongues. Speak so he can understand and speak that which will convict and condemn him. Once he's convicted, judged, and reached, here's his response: "And so falling down on his face he will worship God, and report that God is in you of a truth" (v. 25b). I believe this is Paul's way of indicating that the man has been brought to conversion. The initial response to salvation is worship. Salvation, then, is the source, or basis, of worship.

Is Christian worship simply Christianized Judaism?

If Jesus were to arrive on the scene today and look at the big picture of Christianity, I wonder what kind of things He'd have to say about the "Christian worship" that goes on. A. P. Gibbs, in his book *Worship*, says this: "Much of the so-called 'public worship' in Christendom, is merely a form of Christianized Judaism, and, in some some cases, thinly veiled paganism. . . . In Judaism there was a separate priestly caste who alone could conduct the worship of Israel. In Christendom a man-made priesthood, called the 'clergy,' is essential to its worship, in spite of the plain teaching of the New Testament that all believers are priests. These priests of Judaism wore a distinctive dress, as also does the clergy. Judaism emphasized an earthly sanctuary, or building. In like manner, Christendom makes much of its consecrated 'places of worship,' and miscalls the edifice . . . 'the house of God.' Jewish priests had an altar on which were offered sacrifices to God. Christendom has erected 'altars' in these ornate buildings, before which candles burn and incense is offered and, in many cases, on which a wafer is kept, which is looked upon as the body of Christ! It is hardly necessary to say that all this copying of Judaism is absolutely foreign to the teaching of the New Testament.

"Thus Christendom has initiated its own specially educated and ordained priesthood, whose presence is indispensable to 'administer the sacraments.' These men, robed in gorgeous vestments, from within a roped off 'sanctuary,' stand before a bloodless 'altar,' with a background of burning candles, crosses and smoking incense, and 'conduct the worship' for the laity. With the use of an elaborate

49

prepared ritual, with stereotyped prayers, and responses from the audience, the whole service proceeds smoothly and with mechanical precision. It is a marvel of human invention and ingenuity, with an undoubted appeal to the esthetic; but a tragic and sorry substitute for the spiritual worship which our Lord declared that His Father sought from His redeemed children." ([Walterick: Kansas City, n.d.] pp. 97-98.)

I believe if Jesus were to arrive on the scene today, He would indict all the ritualistic worship—similar to the Judaistic worship of His day—as well as the less elaborate, less ornate, less sophisticated, shallow, indifferent, Samaritan-type worship. He would indict these forms of worship and would accept only the true worship of those who "worship the Father in spirit and in truth" (John 4:23b).

Before we go on to the next major point, let me set the scene for you. In John 4:3, it says that Jesus "left Judaea, and departed again into Galilee." But according to verse 4, He had to go through Samaria. Why? Because Jesus had a divine appointment with a special woman. God was seeking her out to be a true worshiper, so He sent Jesus out of the normal route to Galilee from Judaea (for a Jew) and had Him go through Samaria.

Let's follow the narrative of this divine encounter, starting in verse 5: "Then cometh he to a city of Samaria, which is called Sychar, near to the plot of ground that Jacob gave to his son, Joseph. Now Jacob's well was there. Jesus, therefore, being wearied with his journey, sat by the well; and it was about the sixth hour. There cometh a woman of Samaria to draw water. Jesus saith unto her, Give me to drink. For his disciples were gone away unto the city to buy food. Then saith the woman of Samaria unto him, How is it that thou, being a Jew, askest drink of me, who am a woman of Samaria? For the Jews have no dealings with the Samaritans [lit. 'the Jews don't use the same vessels as the Samaritans']. Jesus answered, and said unto her, If thou knewest the gift of God, and who it is that saith to thee, Give me to drink, thou wouldest have asked of him, and he would have given thee living water. The woman saith unto him, Sir, thou hast nothing to draw with, and the well is deep; from where, then, hast thou that living water? Art thou greater than our father, Jacob, who gave us the well, and drank from it himself, and his sons, and his cattle? Jesus answered, and said unto her, Whosoever drinketh of this water shall thirst again; but whosoever drinketh of the water that I shall give him shall never thirst, but the water that I shall give him shall be in him a well of water springing up into everlasting life. The woman saith unto him, Sir, give me this water, that I thirst not, neither come here to draw."

We really don't know whether this woman's response to Christ was in the terms of His parable or whether she was still on a literal level talking about real water. But I personally feel that she knew He was talking about something other than physical water. After all, what kind of water could give eternal life?

Continuing on, in verse 16, Jesus goes right to the heart of the matter—a problem that hindered Him from giving this living water to her. Here's how He brought this problem up: "Jesus saith unto her, Go, call thy husband, and come here. The woman answered, and said, I have no husband. Jesus said unto her,

Thou hast well said, I have no husband; for thou hast had five husbands, and he whom thou now hast is not thy husband; that saidst thou truly. The woman said unto him, Sir, I perceive that thou art a prophet."

Why did she perceive that Jesus was a prophet? Three reasons: (1) She understood that He was speaking of supernatural truth. Even though it appears, in her response to Him in verse 15, that she's thinking in terms of the physical, I believe she saw Him as a prophet because she understood, to some extent, that He was speaking about spiritual things; (2) He went right to the core and indicted her for her sin; and (3) He knew secrets that only God could have revealed. Here was a man who spoke of spiritual realities, dealt with sin, and knew things that only God could reveal.

Once she perceived that the man she was talking to was obviously a prophet, verse 20 implies that her first reaction was, "I've got to get my life right! I want to worship, but I don't know where to go! My people say to go up to Mount Gerizim, but Your people say to go down to Jerusalem. Where do I go to worship?" Then, in verses 21-24, Jesus basically says, "Lady, in just a little while, there isn't going to be an 'up here' and a 'down there'—that's not the issue. The issue is that you worship the Father in spirit and in truth."

Now, all of that is the background to this marvelous passage in John 4:20-24 on true spiritual worship. This woman of Samaria probably felt profound conviction of her sin. Her conscience was pricked, her soul was pierced, and she wanted to deal with her sin—but she didn't know where to go. She believed, like the rest of the people of that day, that worship was something that was done at a prescribed place and a set time—only she wasn't sure which place was the right place. So Jesus responded to her dilemma—giving us this great passage on worship.

As we look at John 4:20-24, I want to discuss:

III. THE OBJECT OF WORSHIP

What is the object of our worship? Well, Jesus tells us to "worship the Father" (v. 21b), "worship the Father" (v. 23b), and "worship him" (v. 24b). So who are we to worship? The Father. Also, it tells us in verse 24a who He is: "God is a Spirit."

This gives us two aspects to the object of worship—God as Spirit and God as Father. We are to worship God as Spirit which speaks of His essential nature, and God as Father, which speaks of His essential relationship. Both of these are basic to true worship. Let's look at them individually.

A. God as Spirit (His Essential Nature)

1. The spirituality of God

John 4:24a, in the Greek, reads, "Spirit, the God." *Spirit* and *God* are just melted together, making one equal to the other. In other words, God is the God who is the one glorious Spirit. What does it mean that He is Spirit?

a) He cannot be reduced to an image

I believe an examination of Isaiah 40:18-26 will help us understand the essential nature of God as Spirit. Verse 18 begins:

51

"To whom, then, will ye liken God? Or what likeness will ye compare unto him?" In other words, if someone can't deal with the spiritual nature of God, and he's going to reduce Him into an image, what's the image going to look like?

Verse 19 continues, "The workman melteth and casteth an image, and the goldsmith spreadeth it over with gold, and casteth silver chains. He that is so impoverished that he hath no oblation, chooseth a tree that will not rot; he seeketh a skillful workman to prepare a carved image, that shall not be moved. Have ye not known? Have ye not heard? Hath it not been told you from the beginning? Have ye not understood from the foundations of the earth? It is he who sitteth upon the circle of the earth, and the inhabitants thereof are like grasshoppers; who stretcheth out the heavens like a curtain, and spreadeth them out like a tent to dwell in: who bringeth the princes to nothing; he maketh the judges of the earth as vanity. Yea, they shall not be planted; yea, they shall not be sown; yea, their stock shall not take root in the earth; and he shall also blow upon them, and they shall wither, and the whirlwind shall take them away like stubble." In other words, the most important and powerful people in the world are nothing when compared to God.

Verse 25 continues, "To whom, then, will ye liken me, or shall I be equal? saith the Holy One. Lift up your eyes on high, and behold who hath created these things, who bringeth out their host by number; he calleth them all by names by the greatness of his might; for he is strong in power. Not one faileth."

The point of this passage is this: When you try to conceive of God in your mind's eye, or in theological terms, or in biblical terms, you cannot reduce Him to an image. He is Spirit and must be worshiped as such.

b) He cannot be confined to a place

Jeremiah 23:23-24 says, "Am I a God at hand, saith the Lord, and not a God afar off? Can any hide himself in secret places that I shall not see him? saith the Lord. Do not I fill heaven and earth? saith the Lord." In other words, God is not an idol confined to a place. He cannot be confined to a specific place or time. Do you see how important that is in worship? We don't have to go somewhere to worship God, with the thought that He's only there at a specific time. God is Spirit and fills time and space.

(1) Mt. Gerizim/Jerusalem

In John 4:20, the woman of Samaria shows confusion about where to go to worship God. The Samaritans worshiped at Mount Gerizim, and the Jews worshiped at Jerusalem. So Jesus responds to her in verse 21: "Woman,

52

believe me, the hour cometh, when ye shall neither in this mountain, nor yet at Jerusalem, worship the Father."

Verse 21 is so loaded with truth that it can be interpreted telescopically. *Individually,* Jesus could be saying, "Lady, you're about to enter into a relationship with God through Me that will enable you to worship God in your heart, not in a geographical location." *Historically,* He could be saying, "The time is coming when Jerusalem will be destroyed, and nothing is up on that mountain anyway." And in its *widest possible interpretation,* He could be saying, "I am going to bring about the redemptive work on the cross of Calvary that will eliminate all that is in any way associated with the old covenant—true or false."

Then, in verse 23*a*, Jesus says, "But the hour cometh, and now is." That's a fascinating statement. Something is future, and yet present. What did He mean by that? Well, basically He was saying, "I'm standing in a transition. In one hand I have the old covenant, and in the other hand I have the new covenant. The hour is coming, and is already here (because I'm here), when the old covenant will be gone and the new covenant will be here. In that new covenant, there will be no place—no Jerusalem—to worship in." And just to make sure that nobody would get confused, God wiped out Jerusalem in A.D. 70.

What Jesus was saying, then, is that God must be worshiped as Spirit, and as such, He is everywhere. He can't be confined to a place—Mount Gerizim or Jerusalem.

What is the "new and living way"?

In our Lord's discussion with the woman of Samaria in John 4, I believe He predicted the end of the whole Jewish ceremonial system of worship (vv. 21*b*, 23*a*)—the old covenant. This was also dramatized in one great climactic event that occurred when Jesus died on the cross. The veil of the Temple was torn in two from top to bottom, exposing the holy of holies (Matt. 27:51). This indicated that the whole ceremonial system had ended.

The epistle of Hebrews also teaches that the sacrifice of Christ on the cross ended the Jewish ceremonial system, giving us a new kind of worship. Look at chapter 10. Verse 4 says, "For it is not possible that the blood of bulls and of goats should take away sins." In other words, the sacrificial system couldn't do it. Further, verses 11-12 tell us: "And every priest standeth daily ministering and offering often the same sacrifices, which can never take away sins; but this man [Christ], after he had offered one sacrifice for sins forever, sat down on the right hand of God." The fact that He sat down indicates that His work was finished. Verses 14-22*a* continue: "For by one offering he hath perfected forever them that are sanctified. And the Holy Spirit also is a witness to us; for after he had said before, This is the covenant that I will make with them after those days, saith the Lord: I will put my laws into their hearts, and in their minds will I write them, and their sins and iniquities will I remember no more. Now where remission of these is, there is no more offering for sin [i.e., the sacrificial system was over when Christ died]. Having therefore, brethren, boldness to enter into the holiest by the blood of Jesus, by a new and living way [not the old way of dead animals—the old way of ceremonial sacrifice], which he hath consecrated for us, through the veil, that is to say, his flesh, and having an high priest over the house of God, let us draw near with a true heart in full assurance of faith."

You see, it's because of the work of Christ on the cross that we become a worshiping people. The old ceremonial systems are gone. Christ is the "new and living way."

So the issue isn't the *place* of worship; the issue is *who* is worshiped. And He must be worshiped as a Spirit—not confined to a specific geographical location such as Mount Gerizim or Jerusalem.

(2) The Tabernacle/Temple

You say, "John, how can you say that God was to be worshiped as a Spirit, everywhere, when the Jews had the Temple?" The Temple was only a resident symbol to stimulate their worship as a way of life. If you don't understand that, you miss the whole point of the Temple. It was a symbol, not a reality! You say, "Didn't the Shekinah glory of God dwell between the wings of the cherubim at the top of the mercy seat, on the Ark of the Covenant, in the holy of holies?" Sure, but do you think that the omnipresent God confined Himself to the Tabernacle or to the Temple and wasn't present anywhere else? Of course not! The Shekinah glory was only a symbol of His presence. Only the Jews who were ignorant confined God to the Temple.

Now, at times, God did express or reveal Himself in a place. Very often God would meet one of the patriarchs in a unique place, and the patriarch would build an altar there, wouldn't he? But just because God was in one place, at one time, for one special reason, that doesn't mean that He wasn't everywhere else at the same time. The Tabernacle and the Temple were just to stimulate them to a life of worship.

So, the issue isn't *where* we worship. In fact, it isn't even *when* we worship (Col. 2:16-17; Gal. 4:9-10). God is Spirit, and He must be worshiped in a spiritual way.

Focusing on the Facts

1. What is acceptable worship the direct result of? How do Luke 19:10 and John 4:23 relate to each other (see p. 47)?

2. Of what is Psalm 22:1-21 a prophetic picture? What response follows that in verses 22-27 (see p. 47)?

3. After giving Israel the Ten Commandments, what else did God give them, according to Exodus 20:22-26? Why (see p. 48)?

4. What did the Old Testament sacrifices make possible? Explain what the sacrifice of Christ did (see p. 48).

5. Explain the relationship of Isaiah 52 and 53 to chapter 66 with regard to worship (see p. 49).

6. What elements of worship in many churches are merely copies from the rituals of Judaism? Why are such practices no longer valid (see pp. 49-50)?

7. From a divine perspective, why did Jesus go through Samaria on His way to Galilee in John 4 (see p. 50)?

8. Why did the Samaritan woman perceive that Jesus was a prophet? What was her first reaction to that realization (implied in verse 20; see p. 51)?

9. What should be the object of all worship (see p. 51)?

10. Can God be represented by an image? Support your answer using the reasoning of Isaiah 40:18-25 (see pp. 51-52).

11. How should the fact that God cannot be confined to a specific place or time affect our worship (see p. 52)?

12. With regard to worship, what transition was Jesus standing in during His earthly ministry (see p. 53)?

13. What did Jesus predict the end of in John 4:21 and 23? How was that ending dramatized at His death (see p. 53)?

14. Explain the "new and living way" (Heb. 10:20) that Jesus opened up (Heb. 10:11-22; see pp. 53-54).

15. What was the Temple meant to be in Judaism? What was the Shekinah of God a symbol of (see p. 54)?

16. Did God ever manifest Himself in other locations? Give an example (see p. 54).

Pondering the Principles

1. When you first understood the significance of Christ's death, what was your response? Do you regularly contemplate the death of Christ? Read 1 Corinthians 11:23-26. What is the purpose of eating the bread and drinking the cup of Communion? Does your church have that focus? What do you personally think about during the times when your church celebrates Communion? Some churches overemphasize the suffering of Christ in Communion, and others fail to communicate the significance of Communion altogether. The next time your participate in the Lord's Table, make sure that you recall the importance of the Lord's death, and thank Him for the eternal benefit you derive from that incredible act of love. Meditate on the words of Charles Wesley, who wrote "And Can It Be That I Should Gain?":

> And can it be that I should gain
> An int'rest in the Savior's blood?

Died He for me, who caused His pain?
For me, who Him to death pursued?

Amazing love! How can it be
That Thou, my God, shouldst die for me?
Amazing love! How can it be
That Thou, my God, shouldst die for me?

2. Read Hebrews 10:10-22. How was Christ able to make Christians holy in the sight of God (vv. 10-13)? How long will the perfection of our salvation last (v. 14)? What does the forgiveness of sins give to those who are under the new covenant (v. 19)? We can enter the presence of God now through prayer as we await our entrance into heaven. Are you actively exercising your privilege of prayer? Praise the Lord that He has opened the door for sinful man to be made holy that he may fellowship with Him for eternity!

5
True Worship—Part 5

Outline

Introduction

Review
I. The Importance of Worship
II. The Source (Basis) of Worship
III. The Object of Worship
   A. God as Spirit (His Essential Nature)
      1. The spirituality of God
         a) He cannot be reduced to an image
         b) He cannot be confined to a place
            (1) Mt. Gerizim/Jerusalem
            (2) The Tabernacle/Temple

Lesson
         a) Acts 7:46-50
         b) Acts 17:24-25
      2. The holiness of God
         a) A response of godly fear
            (1) Psalm 96:2-9
            (2) Hebrews 12:28*b*-29
            (3) Isaiah 6:1-8
            (4) 2 Timothy 2:22
         b) A response of thanksgiving
            (1) His mercy extended
            (2) His justice exemplified

Introduction

I believe there's a very serious problem in the church today. Little emphasis is given to the matter of worship. Today's church doesn't focus itself on true worship. A. W. Tozer, of a past generation, said, "Worship is the missing jewel in the evangelical church." If that was true in his time, it is equally or more true in ours. America's twentieth-century church doesn't know how to worship. For this reason, we're looking at the subject of worship and calling the people of God to commit themselves to acceptable, true, spiritual worship.

Review

I. THE IMPORTANCE OF WORSHIP

II. THE SOURCE (BASIS) OF WORSHIP

In our last lesson we ended in the midst of discussing the third major point in our outline:

III. THE OBJECT OF WORSHIP

Who is it that we worship? It's not enough to just worship. The object of our worship must be clearly understood. There are people all over the world who worship—and have been throughout all of human history. They do not, however, worship the right object. Our Lord, in John 4, clearly instructs that there is only one object of worship. He says, "Worship the Father" (v. 21*b*), "Worship the Father" (v. 23*b*), and "Worship him" (v. 24*b*). So we are to worship the Father. Also, in verse 24*a* Jesus says, "God is a Spirit." The One we are to worship, then, is defined to us in two terms: *Spirit* and *Father*. *Spirit* speaks of His essential nature, and *Father* speaks of His essential relationship.

A. God as Spirit (His Essential Nature)

    1. The spirituality of God

        a) He cannot be reduced to an image (see pp. 51-52)

        b) He cannot be confined to a place (see pp. 52-54)
            (1) Mt. Gerizim/Jerusalem (see pp. 52-53)
            (2) The Tabernacle/Temple (see p. 54)

Lesson

We left off last time discussing the misunderstanding that many people have in believing that God lived in and was confined to the Tabernacle and, later, to the Temple. Well, in a unique sense God's presence was in those places—but not in a limiting sense. Although His presence was there, He was also everywhere else. The Temple, the Tabernacle, the holy place, and the Holy of Holies were all symbols. In fact, the whole ceremonial system was symbolic and existed in order that man might perceive God in the symbol. It was to be the starting place of their perception of God, not the ending. They were to see beyond the symbols to the reality of the living God.

Let me give you some scriptural illustrations.

        (*a*) Acts 7:46-50—In Acts 7, Stephen preached a great sermon in which he recited much of the history of the people of God. In verse 46, he says that David "found favor before God, and desired to find a tabernacle for the God of Jacob. But Solomon built him an house."

Now, the fact that Solomon built God a great Temple did not mean that God was confined to that Temple as we might be confined to a house. This is confirmed by verses 48-50: "Nevertheless, the Most High dwelleth not in temples made with hands, as saith the prophet, Heaven is my throne, and earth is my footstool. What house will ye build me? saith the Lord. Or what is the place of my rest? Hath not my hand made all these things?"

Only an ignorant Jew would have perceived that God was limited to the Temple. An understanding Jew knew that the Temple was only a symbol in the midst of the people as a reminder of the eternal presence of the eternal omnipresent God. In fact, they knew that from the very beginning. In Deuteronomy 6, they were given the most basic truth of their religion: "The Lord our God is one Lord" (v. 4). God then told them to teach it diligently to their children and to speak of it continually, "When thou sittest in thine house, and when thou walkest by the way, and when thou liest down, and when thou risest up" (v. 7b). In other words, no matter where they were, or what they were doing, they were to be aware of the eternal, living, one, holy God. The Temple was only a reminder. The ceremonial sacrificial system was only to be a prodder of their conscience, causing them to turn their hearts toward the true and living God. The symbol was to produce in them the reality of a life committed to worshiping God. It was never intended to be the end, only the means.

(b) Acts 17:24-25—Paul, speaking to the philosophers in Athens, said, "God, who made the world and all things in it, seeing that he is Lord of heaven and earth, dwelleth not in temples made with hands, neither is worshiped with men's hands, as though He needed anything, seeing he giveth to all life, and breath, and all things." In other words, the God who extends through all of time, space, infinity, and eternity cannot be confined or limited. Therefore, He is to be worshiped at all times, in all places, by all people.

The pagan perspective of limiting God

The Syrians called the God of Israel "gods of the hills" (1 Kings 20:23). This reflected their own idolatrous perspective, because their gods were the gods of the valleys. They had built groves for their gods in the valleys and felt that they were confined to those groves. This pagan perspective of God being confined to a specific place may have influenced the confused worship of the Samaritans who thought that God was confined to Mount Gerizim. But the truth of the matter is that God is Spirit and is to be worshiped in the fullness of His spiritual presence.

Outward symbol versus inward reality

In Jeremiah 7:21-23, the Lord gives Jeremiah a message to speak to His sinful people: "Thus saith the Lord of hosts, the God of Israel, Put your burnt offerings unto your sacrifices, and eat flesh. For I spoke not unto your fathers, nor commanded them in the day that I brought them out of the land of Egypt, concerning burnt offerings or sacrifices." In other words, "Put that away. That wasn't what I was after. That was only a symbol of the reality!" Verse 23 continues, "But this thing commanded I them, saying, Obey my voice, and I will be your God, and ye shall be my people; and walk in all the ways that I have commanded you, that it may be well unto you." The sacrifices weren't an end in themselves, they were only symbols, visible reminders of God's presence.

But all that was in the old covenant. The new covenant ended the ceremonial symbols and the symbol of the Temple. Why? Because the new temple became the believer in whom the living Spirit of God dwelt, and that Spirit of God became the prodder of true worship. Worship was no longer prodded by an outward symbol, it became an inward reality. We who are of the new covenant possess the Spirit of God and together form the living temple of God. The external reminder to worship, which occurred when the Israelites camped around the Tabernacle, now occurs internally through the prompting of the Holy Spirit in the life of every believer.

So, God is to be worshiped as a living Spirit—anywhere, everywhere, at all times, by all people. And when it's said that the basic feature of Christian living is a worshiping life, that's exactly what is meant. Worship is the bottom line. "For we are the circumcision," said Paul, "who worship God in the spirit, and rejoice in Christ Jesus, and have no confidence in the flesh" (Phil. 3:3).

Now, if we are to worship God as Spirit, then we must define His nature. It's important for us to worship the God who is Spirit in terms of how He is revealed in Scripture. And I believe the one attribute which most sums up the nature of God is:

2. The holiness of God

God is holy, and He must be worshiped as holy. His holiness can be defined as "His unique otherness" or "His unlikeness to the human creature." He is flawless, without error, without sin, without mistake, and fully righteous—utterly holy. The basic comprehension for true worship is that God is holy.

There's a lot of well-meaning effort today and a lot of supposed worship going on that does not regard God as holy—and thus falls short. There are a lot of nice songs being sung, nice feelings being felt, nice thoughts being thought, and nice emotions being expressed—but not in terms of the holiness of God. So these "nice" things may be little more than emotional exercises that make one feel good.

God must be worshiped as holy, and the perception of His holiness produces:

a) A response of godly fear

(1) Psalm 96:2-9—"Sing unto the Lord, bless his name; show forth his salvation from day to day. Declare his glory among the nations, his wonders among all peoples. For the Lord is great, and greatly to be praised; he is to be feared above all gods. For all the gods of the nations are idols; but the Lord made the heavens. Honor and majesty are before him; strength and beauty are in his sanctuary. Give unto the Lord, O ye kindreds of the peoples; give unto the Lord glory and strength. Give unto the Lord the glory due unto his name; bring an offering, and come into his courts."

After all of this worship and praise, we come to a key statement in verse 9. Here is the attitude or perspective of worship; "Oh, worship the Lord in the beauty of holiness; fear before him, all the earth." *Holiness can never be perceived apart from fear.* Why? Because if you perceive God as utterly holy, you will in turn perceive yourself as utterly unholy. This will produce a sense of fear, because a holy God has a right to a holy reaction against an unholy creation. So, the true spirit of worship is an overwhelming sense of unholiness in the presence of a holy God.

Just so you don't think the concept of worshiping God with holiness and fear is just an Old Testament concept, look at:

(2) Hebrews 12:28*b*-29—"Serve [or 'worship'] God acceptably with reverence and godly fear; for our God is a consuming fire."

(3) Isaiah 6:1-8—Isaiah went to the Temple to worship the Lord. King Uzziah had died after fifty-two years on the throne, and the Northern Kingdom was about to go into captivity as a judgment for their sin. Isaiah saw the demise of his people, and he sensed the problem in his nation, so he rushed into the presence of God to worship.

In verse 1, we find that he had a vision of God in which He was majestically lifted up and surrounded by seraphim— the guardians of God's holiness. Two of the seraphim's wings were used for service, and four of them were used for worship (v. 2). In verse 3, the seraphim are worshiping God and crying back and forth to each other, saying, "Holy, holy, holy, is the Lord of hosts; the whole earth is full of his glory."

As Isaiah worshiped God, he perceived His holiness—holiness that causes God to react against sin—and he responds in verse 5, "Then said I, Woe is me! For I am undone [i.e., disintegrating, falling apart, going to pieces], because I am a man of unclean lips, and I dwell in the midst of a people of unclean lips." He was overwhelmed with his sinfulness. All he could see was his sin. Even though he had the cleanest mouth of all of them, when he saw himself as compared to God, he couldn't see any goodness in himself. What caused this stark comparison? "For mine eyes have seen the King, the Lord of hosts."

Now, you may not have a vision like this, nor may I, but, nonetheless, the lesson is true that when we enter into the presence of God, if we truly see God, we see Him as holy, holy, holy. We are then faced with a sense of our utter unholiness. If you have never worshiped God with a broken and contrite spirit, then you've never really worshiped God. That's the proper response when entering the presence of a holy God.

Holiness inspires fear, and Isaiah was afraid. Why? Because he knew that a holy God had every right to react against an unholy sinner. He knew that God had every right to judge him and to take his life on the spot.

My heart is concerned that there's a lot of flippancy going on in Christianity today in entering into the presence of God. God has become so casual in our thinking—so human, so buddy-buddy—that we don't understand the whole perspective of His utter holiness. We don't understand that God is a consuming fire and that He has a holy indignance against sin. We must consider that if we flippantly rush into His presence with lives unattended to by repentance, confession, and cleansing by the Spirit, then we are vulnerable to that holy reaction. It is only by His grace that we breathe another breath, is it not? He has every reason to take our life! Why? "For the wages of sin is death" (Rom. 6:23a). So Isaiah had the only reaction that a true worshiper could ever have in true worship—humble, broken contrition. He saw himself as a sinner. In the midst of his repentance and confession, an angel came with a coal and purged him (vv. 6-7). Then God told Isaiah that He would send him in His place (v. 8)—revealing a marvelous communion, comradery, and union that takes place between God and a true worshiper through the confession of sin. That's really the spirit of true worship—seeing the holiness of God and becoming overwhelmed with your own unholiness.

(4) 2 Timothy 2:22—In 2 Timothy, Paul is writing to Timothy and instructing him about being a godly man and a faithful

servant of the Lord Jesus Christ. He tells him what is necessary to guard his life for usefulness, talks to him about being "a vessel unto honor, sanctified, and fit for the master's use, and prepared unto every good work" (2:21), and then in 2:22 he says, "Flee also youthful lusts, but follow righteousness, faith, love, peace, with them that call on the Lord out of a pure heart." This last statement is a marvelous insight into true worship—calling upon the Lord out of a pure heart. Now, our hearts are not made pure by our own designs or by our own devices, they are made pure by the confession and the repentance that is experienced when we face a holy God.

What happens when men encounter God's holiness?

In the Old Testament, whenever the people of God encountered God, they usually had a terrifying reaction—they felt afraid, intimidated, and that their lives were in danger. Why? Because they knew they were sinners in the presence of a holy God. For example:

- Abraham—In Genesis 18:27, Abraham entered into God's presence and confessed that he was nothing but "dust and ashes."

- Job—When Job, who was a righteous man (Job 1:8), came to the end of his amazing pilgrimage, he saw God as the sovereign, holy Lord of the universe, and said, "Wherefore I abhor myself, and repent in dust and ashes" (Job 42:6).

- Manoah—When Manoah, the father of Samson, saw the angel of the Lord, he said to his wife, "We shall surely die, because we have seen God" (Judg. 13:22).

- Habakkuk—When Habakkuk heard the voice of the Lord, this was his reaction: "When I heard, my belly trembled; my lips quivered at the voice; rottenness entered into my bones, and I trembled in myself" (Hab. 3:16*a*).

- The restored remnant—When the holy words of God were spoken by Haggai to the restored remnant of Israel, "The people did fear before the Lord" (Hag. 1:12*b*).

- Ezra—In the ninth chapter of Ezra, Ezra goes before the Lord with a broken and contrite heart in the spirit of true worship, and says, "O my God, I am ashamed and blush to lift up my face to thee, my God; for our iniquities are increased over our head, and our trespass is grown up into the heavens" (v. 6). And then he said, "Behold, we are before thee in our trespasses; for we cannot stand before thee because of this" (v.15*b*).

A true worshiper comes into the presence of God with fear—knowing that God has a right to take his life. Even though we are His children and have been redeemed by the blood of Jesus Christ, God still has a right to punish us for sin. Hebrews 12:6 says, "For whom the Lord loveth he chasteneth, and scourgeth every son whom he receiveth."

In the New Testament, when men encountered the holy God in human flesh, they too reacted in fear. For example:

- The disciples—In Mark 4:41, after the disciples saw Jesus still the wind and the sea, it says, "And they feared exceedingly, and said one to another, What manner of man is this, that even the wind and the sea obey him?" You see, they realized that having God in their boat was far worse than the storm outside their boat. Why? Because they had to face His holiness in the power that had been displayed.

- The people of Gerasa—When Jesus cast a multitude of demons out of a man and into a herd of pigs, which all ran violently into a lake and drowned, the people of the country of Gerasenes ran out and "besought him to depart from them; for they were taken with great fear" (Luke 8:37b).

- Peter—In Luke 5, Jesus comes up to Peter, who had been fishing all night without catching anything, and said, "Launch out into the deep, and let down your nets for a draught" (v. 4). Grudgingly, he obeyed. But when he caught so many fish that his nets broke, verse 8 tells us, "He fell down at Jesus' knees, saying, Depart from me; for I am a sinful man, O Lord." All Peter could see, when confronted with the reality of a holy God, was his own sinfulness.

- The Pharisees—I believe one of the reasons that the Pharisees wanted to kill Jesus was because they were so afraid of Him. They were astonished at what He taught and at what He did. They panicked when they saw His power and heard His wisdom.

Jesus traumatized people, because when they knew that God was in their midst, they were immediately confronted with the evil of their hearts.

A true worshiping life is a life of brokenness and contrition—a life that sees sin and confesses continually. You can't live a life of sin throughout the week and then go to church on Sunday thinking you're going to worship the Lord. If God is a spirit and is everywhere at all times, He is to be worshiped that way. And if He is holy, we are to worship Him with a sense of fear. Why? Because He has a right to chasten our unholiness.

Just to keep the balance, however, the perception of God's holiness also produces:

b) A response of thanksgiving

You say, "Why does God's holiness cause us to live a life of thanksgiving?" Because He doesn't give us what we deserve—He hasn't rendered to us according to our sins. But even His mercy causes us problems. According to Romans 2:4b, "the goodness of God leadeth . . . to repentance." But we get so used to sinning and getting away with it that we just keep sinning. We're so used to God's mercy, grace, and forgiveness that we abuse them.

(1) His mercy extended

God is a holy God. If He wanted to enforce His holiness, all of us would be dead, because Romans 6:23a says, "For the wages of sin is death." Originally, God told Adam that if he disobeyed Him, he would die (Gen. 2:17). God only gave Adam and Eve one prohibition, and if they violated it, they would die. But when they did disobey, God was merciful and spared their lives.

In the beginning, any sin was a capital offense, but by the time of the Mosaic covenant, only thirty-five sins had a capital punishment assigned to them. And in many instances, God acted graciously toward the violators of those sins. For example, David committed sins that had been given the death penalty—over and over again—but God was gracious and merciful and forgave him. Now, there were consequences, but death wasn't one of them.

Another example is the sin of adultery. According to the Mosaic law, if a partner committed adultery in a marriage, the punishment was death. But God in His grace, because of the hardness of men's hearts, provided divorce to spare a life.

God has shown Himself gracious, but that doesn't mean He doesn't care about our sin. It doesn't mean we can run into His presence with sin in our lives, and it doesn't mean we can abuse His mercy. The day may come when He acts in righteous indignation against sin in our lives. And if He does, He has every right to do so. You see, we get so used to mercy, that when God does what is just, we think He is unjust.

(2) His justice exemplified

When somebody dies prematurely, people often say, "How could God let that happen?" When problems arise and life becomes difficult, people say, "How can God allow that to happen?" Well, the question is How can God *not* allow those things to occur when we are sinful people? You see, we look at it backwards!

Many people look at the Bible and ask, "What kind of God sends two bears out to tear up forty-two little children, just because they yelled, 'Baldy, baldy,' at the prophet Elisha (2 Kings 2:23-24)? What kind of God slays two young men, Nadab and Abihu, on the day of their ordination, just because they got a little drunk and fooled around with the Temple incense (Lev. 10:1-2)? What kind of God slays a man who touches the ark to try to keep it from falling off a cart (2 Sam. 6:6-7)? What kind of God gives a man leprosy

65

when he's been a faithful king for fifty-two years—just because he got a little proud (2 Kings 15:1-5)? Why does God punish some and not others? Why did God slay Ananias and Sapphira (Acts 5:1-10)? After all, they gave a gift to the Lord—it just wasn't what they said they'd give. Why did they have to die for that?"

Well, the question isn't, for example, Why did Ananias and Sapphira die? The question is, Why didn't *you* die when you failed to give the Lord something you promised Him? The question isn't, Why did God take the life of someone who committed adultery? The question is, Why doesn't God take the life of *everyone* who commits adultery? You see, it's never a question of God's being unjust, it's only an issue of God's being merciful. Sometimes, when He *does* do what is just, He does it as an illustration, or signpost, to remind men of His holiness and to warn them of His judgment against sin (see 1 Cor. 10:5-12). So, as we look through Scripture and see the times when God acted in a holy way against unholiness, it shows us what God has a right to do. The question isn't, How can God be so unjust? The question is, How can God be so merciful when His holiness is violated? That's the issue!

I've heard people say, "Isn't it awful that some Corinthian Christians actually died because they were coming to the Lord's Table with a sinful life (1 Cor. 11:27-32)?" Well, that's not the issue. The issue is, Why are *we* still alive when *we've* come that way so many times? It's only by His grace.

People say, "Why did God turn Lot's wife into a pillar of salt (Gen. 19:26)?" That isn't the question. The question is, Why doesn't He turn *us* into pillars of salt when we act in a similar worldly fashion and lust after the things of the flesh? You ask, "Why did He swallow up Korah, Dathan, and Abiram in the ground for being disobedient (Num. 16:23-33)?" That isn't the question. The question is, Why doesn't He swallow *us* up in the ground when we're disobedient? We have to see things from the side of God's holiness. God is gracious, but don't let His grace sell short His holiness.

In Luke 13:1-5 some people come to Jesus and tell Him about the Galileans who went into the Temple to offer sacrifices. While they were offering the blood of their sacrifices, Pilate's men came in, sliced them up, and mingled their blood with the blood of the sacrifices. Then the people asked Jesus, "Why did God let that happen? Were they worse sinners than anybody else?" Jesus answered, "I tell you, Nay. But, except ye repent, ye shall

all likewise perish" (v. 3). In other words, "You better get your lives straightened up, or the same thing could happen to you!"

Then the people said, "Well, why did God let that tower in Siloam fall over and kill eighteen victims? What did they do? Were they worse than anybody else?" Jesus answered, "I tell you, Nay. But, except ye repent, ye shall all likewise perish" (v. 5).

You see, the question wasn't, Why did those Galileans get slaughtered? or, Why did those eighteen people get crushed under a falling tower? Jesus showed them the real issue and said, "You had better get your life straightened up, or the same thing could happen to you."

This is all summed up in Hebrews 12:28b-29, which says that we must worship God "acceptably with reverence and godly fear; for our God is a consuming fire." This means that we are to live holy lives before God. We are to live lives of confession and repentance, so that our worship is pleasing and acceptable to God. And we must never go rushing into His presence to worship with unholiness in our lives, lest we receive our just deserts at His hand. While we are thankful for His grace, and we understand His love, we have somehow, in twentieth-century Christianity, missed His holiness—the heart of worship.

God is a living, eternal, glorious, holy, merciful Spirit—the object of our worship. And we must come to worship Him in the contrition, humility, and brokenness of sinners who see themselves against the backdrop of His utter holiness.

F. W. Faber, who has written so many beautiful words, wrote this hymn of praise:

My God, how wonderful Thou art, Thy majesty how bright!
How beautiful Thy mercy-seat in depths of burning light!

How dread are Thine eternal years, O everlasting Lord!
By prostrate spirits, day and night, incessantly adored.

How wonderful, how beautiful the sight of Thee must be,
Thine endless wisdom, boundless power and awful purity!

O how I fear Thee, living God, with deepest, tenderest fears,
And worship Thee with trembling hope and penitential tears!

Yet I may love Thee too, O Lord, Almighty as Thou art,
For Thou hast stooped to ask of me the love of my poor heart.

No earthly father loves like Thee; no mother, e'er so mild,
Bears and forbears as Thou hast done with me, Thy sinful child.

1. Why was the ceremonial system established (see p. 58)?
2. What was the most basic truth of Judaism that was to be continually brought to mind (Deut. 6:4; see p. 59)?
3. What were the symbols of the ceremonial sacrificial system designed to produce in the people (see p. 59)?
4. What was the reality that God sought from His people, according to Jeremiah 7:23? What would be the result of that (see p. 60)?
5. Explain the realities of the new covenant that replaced the symbols of the Old Covenant (see p. 60).
6. What is the one divine attribute that most nearly sums up the nature of God? What does it mean (see p. 60)?
7. What does the perception of God's holiness produce in man? Why (see pp. 61-67)?
8. In the vision of Isaiah 6:1-8, how did Isaiah see himself as compared to God (see p. 62)?
9. Describe the flippant attitude that is common in Christianity today. What must such Christians understand? What reaction should a true worshiper have as a result of that understanding (see p. 62)?
10. Name some people in the Old and New Testaments who encountered God's holiness and describe a typical reaction (see p. 63).
11. Even though Christians have been redeemed by the blood of Christ, does God still have a right to punish us for sin? Support your answer with Scripture (see p. 63).
12. How does the reaction that the Gerasenes (Luke 8:37) and the Pharisees had toward Jesus differ from that of the other people mentioned on page 64?
13. In a positive light, what does the perception of God's holiness cause us to do? Why (see p. 64)?
14. What would happen to men if God wanted to enforce His holiness? Why (see p. 65)?
15. Explain how God had been gracious to David (see p. 65).
16. Under Mosaic law, what punishment did adultery incur? What did God allow so that a life could be spared? Does that mean that His mercy can be abused (see p. 65)?
17. When might we think that God is being unjust? Why? Give an example (see pp. 65-66).
18. How does the demonstration of God's justice serve as a signpost (1 Cor. 10:5-12; see p. 66)?
19. The question isn't, "How can God be so _____?" Rather, the question is, "How can God be so _____ when His _____ is violated?" (see p. 66).

Pondering the Principles

1. Although our finite minds can't comprehend how it is possible, the Trinity resides within every believer. With whom does God make His abode, according to John 14:23? What does God give to those He indwells, according to Romans 8:11? What is the mystery that has been revealed, according to Colossians 1:27? Knowing that God has graciously chosen to dwell in those He has redeemed and has empowered us to live a righteous life and promised that we will someday be glorified, offer to God a prayer of thanksgiving. Make a commitment to viewing everything in your life—temptations to sin against God as well as opportunities to glorify Him—from the perspective of realizing that your body is the temple of God. Meditate on 1 Corinthians 6:17-20 and Ephesians 3:14-21.

2. Most people today have overemphasized God's love to the point of excluding His holiness. But there must be a balance between the two. Those who see only a God of love falsely assume that God would never punish sin. They fail to recognize that God, who is merciful, is also just and must punish those who sin against His holiness. Consider the two great sins of David: his adultery with Bathsheba and the murder of her husband (2 Sam. 11:4, 15); and the census of Israel (1 Chron. 21:1-4), which demonstrated his reliance on his army rather than on God. Though David confessed his sins (Ps. 51; 1 Chron. 21:8, 17), what were the consequences for them (2 Sam. 12:7-18; 1 Chron. 21:9-14)? In spite of those heinous crimes that were met with divine justice, David recognized the mercy that God had graciously bestowed on him. Do you willingly accept the consequences for your own sin? Are you able to see—like David was—God's mercy in the context of His justice? Meditate on his words in Psalm 103:6-14.

6

True Worship—Part 6

Outline

Introduction

Review
I. The Importance of Worship
II. The Source (Basis) of Worship
III. The Object of Worship
   A. God as Spirit (His Essential Nature)

Lesson
   B. God as Father (His Essential Relationship)
      1. The trinitarian designation of God
         a) Jesus' usage of the term "Father"
            (1) John 5:17-18
            (2) John 10:29-33
            (3) John 17:1-5
            (4) Matthew 11:27
            (5) John 14:6-11*a*
         b) The Apostles' understanding of the term "Father"
            (1) Ephesians 1:3*a*
            (2) Ephesians 1:17*a*
            (3) 2 Corinthians 1:3
            (4) Philippians 2:9-11
            (5) Romans 15:6
            (6) 1 Peter 1:3*a*
            (7) 2 John 3
      2. The trinitarian worship of God
         a) The worship of the Son
            (1) Defined in the unity of God
            (2) Demonstrated in the early church
            (3) Declared by the apostle Thomas
         b) The worship of the Holy Spirit
IV. The Sphere (Place) of Worship
   A. The Symbolism of the Old Covenant
   B. The Reality of the New Covenant
      1. The temple of our individual bodies
      2. The temple of our collective assembly

a) Ephesians 2:19-22
b) 1 Peter 2:5a
c) 2 Corinthians 6:16b
d) 1 Corinthians 3:9b, 16-17
e) Hebrews 10:24-25a

Introduction

God seeks true worshipers who will worship Him in a manner which is acceptable to Him. We have seen that worship is the theme of history, stretching from Genesis through the end of Revelation. In the beginning, God created man to worship Him, but man rebelled. Since that rebellion, God has sought to bring man back to the point of true worship. That's the purpose for the redemptive plan.

Now, in order to understand worship, it is important that we have a definition. So, we began this series with a simple definition—*Worship is giving honor to God.* Next we looked at some key points that came out of that definition. First, we saw that worship is *giving* to God, not *getting* from Him. When we get together as God's redeemed people in the congregation of fellowship, we gather for the purpose of worship—not to receive, but to give to God. When a Jew in the old covenant went to worship, he didn't go to take something, he went to give an offering of money as well as a sacrifice. Everything was geared around giving to God.

We also noted in our definition of worship that it is in contrast to ministry. Ministry is that which flows *down* from God to us, but worship is that which flows *up* from us to God. They provide a beautiful balance. In the Old Testament, the prophet spoke the words that came down from God to men; but there was also a priest who spoke up to God on the behalf of men. Ministry and worship must always be held in balance.

Review

I. THE IMPORTANCE OF WORSHIP (see pp. 11-43)

The end of John 4:23 tells us why worship is so important. It's important because the Father seeks true worshipers. If God seeks true worshipers, then true worship is important. In fact, I'm convinced that as Christians, the primary reason for our existence is to worship God. It involves what we *are* (true worshipers) and what we are to *do* (truly worship). Worship is the very core of our existence as those who have been redeemed.

II. THE SOURCE (BASIS) OF WORSHIP (see pp. 47-51)

Again, in John 4:23, we see that the Father seeks true worshipers. The source of worship, then, is the efficacious, irresistible, redemptive seeking of the Father. God is drawing true worshipers into His kingdom. We're redeemed to worship and are transformed into true worshipers. Perhaps the best definition of a Christian is found in Philippians 3:3 where it says that we are those "who worship God in the spirit." Also, according to Hebrews 10:16-25, since Christ has redeemed us, since His sacrifice has perfected us, and since we have been brought into God's presence through a new and living way, our response is to "draw near" to God—to worship Him. We are redeemed to worship.

So the *importance* of worship is seen in God seeking worshipers, and the *source* of worship is seen in God redeeming and saving us to that end.

III. THE OBJECT OF WORSHIP

John 4:20-24 tells us to worship God. But specifically, in verses 21, 23, and 24, Jesus says to worship God as Spirit and as Father.

A. God as Spirit (His Essential Nature)

We've already discussed this point at length (see pp. 51-72), but before we continue, let me refresh your memory. God is Spirit, and as such, He cannot be confined to a building, a temple, a grove, or a mountain. In other words, God cannot be confined to a place (see pp. 52-54). Also, because God is Spirit, He cannot be reduced to an image made with hands out of wood, brass, gold, silver, or any other substance (see pp. 51-52). God is beyond being confined to a place or being reduced to an image, because He is an ever-living, ever-present, eternal Spirit—pervading the full universe and on into endless eternity with His conscious presence.

Now, since God is Spirit and is everywhere at all times, our worship of Him is to be a way of life. In Acts 17:28a, Paul said, "For in him we live, and move, and have our being." And since we move in the midst of His spiritual presence, worship is fitting and proper at all times. We don't have to wait to walk into a church to worship, nor do we have to wait until our heads are bowed and our minds consciously drawn into God's throne room. God is everywhere at all times and is therefore to be worshiped everywhere at all times. This is the seeking Father's desire and can only be fulfilled by those of us who have been redeemed.

We worship God as the eternal, omnipresent Spirit, but we can't stop there, because once in verse 21 and twice in verse 23, Jesus makes reference to worshiping "the Father."

Lesson

Now we'll pick up where we left off:

B. God as Father (His Essential Relationship)

I think most people have misunderstood the concept of God as Father here in John 4. Usually when we see the term *Father* in reference to God, we immediately think of Him as *our* loving Father. Seeing the term in that way, Jesus would be saying, "Worship God as a vast, omnipresent, eternal Spirit, but also as an intimate, loving, personal Father." Now, while it's true that God is our loving Father and that we are His children, that *isn't* what is being discussed in John 4. That is *not* the issue, nor is it the emphasis that Jesus is making. The emphasis here is:

72

1. The trinitarian designation of God

   God is Father, Son, and Holy Spirit. He is three Persons in one—the Trinity. And it is in this trinitarian sense that God is designated here as "the Father." It is not primarily referring to us as His children, it is referring to His essential relationship within the Trinity.

   Now watch this carefully. God is presented as the Father of the Son—and the Son is the Lord Jesus Christ. So when we worship God as Father, we're not worshiping Him vaguely as the Father of all mankind (as the liberals might say), we're worshiping Him as the Father of the Lord Jesus Christ. God cannot be worshiped apart from this designation.

   a) Jesus' usage of the term "Father"

      In the New Testament, whenever God is discussed as Father, it is primarily as the Father of Jesus Christ. Every time that Jesus spoke to God, He addressed Him as Father—except when sin separated them at the cross (Matt. 27:46). You say, "What did Jesus mean when He referred to God as His Father?" I *don't* believe that He was emphasizing His *submission*, as a son submits to his father; nor do I believe that He was emphasizing His *generation*, as a son descends from his father. I believe that He was emphasizing His *sameness of essence*, as a son is with his father. If Jesus is the Son and God is the Father, then they are the same essence. That is the heart and soul of the relationship that Jesus constantly expresses with the Father. He is emphasizing the sameness of essence, the oneness of nature. Therefore, *God can never be worshiped unless He is worshiped as the Father of the Lord Jesus Christ.*

      Let me give you some examples that show that when Jesus referred to God as His Father, He was stating His deity, His equality with God.

      (1) John 5:17-18—Jesus answered the Jews who were persecuting Him for healing someone on the Sabbath and said, "My Father worketh hitherto, and I work." In other words, He calls the first person of the Trinity His Father and then says, "We work together." Verse 18 then tells us how the Jews perceived His comment: "Therefore, the Jews sought the more to kill him, because he not only had broken the Sabbath, but said also that God was his Father, making himself equal with God." They were right on target, because that's exactly what Jesus was saying. Whenever Jesus called God His Father, He was speaking of their equality of essence, of nature, of deity.

      (2) John 10:29-33—Jesus said, "My Father, who gave them to me, is greater than all, and no man is able to pluck them out of my Father's hand. I and my Father are one. Then

73

the Jews took up stones again to stone him. Jesus answered them, Many good works have I shown you from my Father; for which of those works do ye stone me? The Jews answered him, saying, For a good work we stone thee not, but for blasphemy; and because that thou, being a man, makest thyself God."

You see, when Jesus said that God was His Father, the Jews knew that Jesus was referring to His sameness of essence—His deity. They knew He was claiming to be equal with God.

(3) John 17:1-5—Jesus prayed to His Father and said, "Father, the hour is come; glorify thy Son, that thy Son also may glorify thee. As thou has given him power over all flesh, that he should give eternal life to as many as thou hast given him. And this is life eternal, that they might know thee, the only true God, and Jesus Christ, whom thou has sent. I have glorified thee on the earth; I have finished the work which thou gavest me to do. And now, O Father, glorify thou me with thine own self with the glory which I had with thee before the world was."

Here, Jesus equated Himself with the Father and then asked for the full glory that He had prior to the incarnation. He was equal with God, and His references to God as His Father were statements of His deity (cf. vv. 11, 21-25).

(4) Matthew 11:27—Jesus said, "All things are delivered unto me by my Father, and no man knoweth the Son, but the Father; neither knoweth any man the Father, except the Son, and he to whomsoever the Son will reveal him."

Here in this marvelous passage, the Lord again presents the unique, essential oneness of the Father and the Son. There is an intimacy of knowledge between the Father and the Son that is not available to human perception, because they are one.

(5) John 14:6-11a—"Jesus saith unto him, I am the way, the truth, and the life; no man cometh unto the Father, but by me. If ye had known me, ye should have known my Father also; and from henceforth ye know him, and have seen him. Philip saith unto him, Lord, show us the Father, and it sufficeth us. Jesus saith unto him, Have I been such a long time with you, and yet hast thou not known me, Philip? He that hath seen me hath seen the Father; and how sayest thou then, Show us the Father? Believest thou not that I am in the Father, and the Father in me? The words that I speak unto you, I speak not myself; but the Father that dwelleth in me, he doeth the works. Believe me that I am in the Father, and the Father in me." The Father and the Son are one.

So, going back to John 4, when Jesus calls God Father, it's not *our* Father that He has in mind; it's *His* Father. It's a blatant, outright statement of His deity—His equality with God.

You say, "Why are you going through all of this, John?" Primarily because there are people who claim to worship God as the eternal, living Spirit who is everywhere present and might even claim to worship Him as their Father. But if they deny that Jesus Christ is the same as God the Father in essence, their worship is unacceptable. No one can acceptably worship God as Spirit without also worshiping God as the Father of the Lord Jesus Christ. God cannot be defined or worshiped in any other terms. Anyone who denies the deity of Christ, yet claims to worship God, is a liar—because God and Christ are one.

b) The Apostles' understanding of the term "Father"

Throughout the Epistles, God is worshiped and identified as the Father of the Lord Jesus Christ.

(1) Ephesians 1:3*a*—Paul began one of the great statements of glory offered to God (one sentence that extends from verse 3 to verse 14) by saying, "Blessed be the God and Father of our Lord Jesus Christ." You see, that is how God is known.

(2) Ephesians 1:17*a*—In Paul's great prayer, he prayed to "the God of our Lord Jesus Christ, the Father of glory."

(3) 2 Corinthians 1:3—Paul said, "Blessed be God, even the Father of our Lord Jesus Christ, the Father of mercies, and the God of all comfort."

(4) Philippians 2:9-11—"Wherefore, God also hath highly exalted him, and given him a name which is above every name, that at the name of Jesus every knee should bow, of things in heaven, and things in earth, and things under the earth, and that every tongue should confess that Jesus Christ is Lord, to the glory of God, the Father."

(5) Romans 15:6—"That ye may with one mind and one mouth glorify God, even the Father of our Lord Jesus Christ." God cannot be worshiped apart from a recognition that Jesus Christ, His Son, is equal to God. That's His deity.

(6) 1 Peter 1:3*a*—Peter wrote, "Blessed be the God and Father of our Lord Jesus Christ."

(7) 2 John 3—John wrote, "Grace be with you, mercy, and peace from God, the Father, and from the Lord Jesus Christ, the Son of the Father, in truth and love."

The point is this—God is not just a floating spirit in whom anybody can sort of plug into anywhere they want, with any particular form they want. God is eternal, vast, and ever-present—to be worshiped at all times, by all people. But the only way someone can come to God is to come to Him as the Father of our Lord Jesus Christ. That's why Jesus had to say, "No man cometh unto the Father, but by me" (John 14:6*b*). God can't be worshiped apart from Jesus Christ.

2. The trinitarian worship of God

   a) The worship of the Son

   John 5:23 gives the logical conclusion to Jesus' equality with God. "That all men should honor [or 'worship'] the Son, even as they honor the Father. He that honoreth not the Son honoreth not the Father, who hath sent him." Did you get that? We're not only to worship the Father, we're also to worship the Son.

   (1) Defined in the unity of God

   Somebody once came to me and said, "I've been taught that it's blasphemous to pray to anyone but the Father. Is that true?" I said, "No, that's not true. It sounds like somebody has just gotten a little bit of knowledge, twisted a few scriptures, and is trying to pass himself off as a Bible teacher." We can't worship God the Father unless we worship the Son. We can't even come before God the Father unless we come in the name of the Son. If we pray to the Father, we're praying to the Son—they're one and the same. If we honor the Father, we're praising the Son. They come together—there's no way to isolate them. Therefore, without Jesus Christ, no one worships at all! We have every right to go to the Son, to praise the Son, to petition the Son, just as we would the Father. We're called upon to worship the Son.

   (2) Demonstrated in the early church

   From the earliest years of the church, Christ was recognized as Lord. He was confessed as Lord in baptism (e.g., Rom. 6:3-4; Gal. 3:26-27), invoked as Lord in the Christian assembly (e.g., Eph. 3:10-12; 2 Tim. 1:2*b*), worshiped as Lord in anticipation of the day when every knee should bow (e.g., Rom. 14:8-12; Phil. 2:9-11), and petitioned as Lord in time of need (e.g., Heb. 4:14-16; 1 John 5:14-15). The bottom line in all worship is that Jesus Christ is Lord—that's fundamental.

   (3) Declared by the apostle Thomas

   When Thomas saw Jesus after the resurrection, he declared, "My Lord and my God" (John 20:28). He had the proper perspective of worship. God is to be worshiped, but only as He is perceived to be one and the same with His Son. They are both to receive honor.

So when we gather we are to worship the Father and the Son. What about the Holy Spirit?

b) The worship of the Holy Spirit

There's nothing in Scripture that directly tells us to worship the Holy Spirit. However, all worship is energized in the power of the Spirit. It is the Spirit who allows us to come into God's presence and cry, "Abba, Father" (Rom. 8:15; Gal 4:6). It is in the Spirit's power and presence that we have access to worship God. He is a vital part of worship, and we must never deny that reality.

I would also add that since the Spirit is equal to the Son and the Father, He's worthy to be worshiped also. Although Scripture doesn't tell us to worship Him, it's a necessary observation. The Holy Spirit is called the "Spirit of God" in many passages (e.g., Matt. 3:16; 12:28; Rom. 8:9, 14; 15:19; 1 Cor. 2:11, 14; 3:16; 6:11; 7:40; 12:3; 2 Cor. 3:3; Eph. 4:30; 1 John 4:2) as well as the "Spirit of Christ" (e.g., Rom. 8:9; 1 Pet. 1:11). The Holy Spirit is the radiation of God the Father and God the Son and, as such, is worthy of worship. So, don't hesitate to worship the Spirit along with the Father and the Son. However, realize that in the uniqueness of the Spirit's ministry in the church age, He calls us to worship the Son, and the Son calls us to worship the Father—even though all are worthy to be worshiped.

So who is the object of worship according to John 4:20-24? God who is Spirit—not some vague, floating, undefined spirit, but the God who is the Father. The Father of whom? All mankind? No. The Father of the Lord Jesus Christ—one in essence with Him. It is fitting as we worship the Father that our hearts go out in worship to Jesus Christ as well.

A prophetic picture of worship

A marvelous scene depicting the worship of the Son is found in Revelation 14:1-3. The apostle John, describing a vision of the future, says, "And I looked and, lo, a Lamb [cf. Rev. 13:8; John 1:29] stood on Mount Zion [which, to a Jew, was a symbol of heaven], and with him an hundred forty and four thousand, having his Father's name written in their foreheads. And I heard a voice from heaven, like the voice of many waters, and like the voice of a great thunder; and I heard the voice of harpers harping with their harps. And they sang, as it were, a new song before the throne, and before the four living creatures and the elders; and no man could learn that song but the hundred and forty and four thousand, who were redeemed from the earth."

What a picture of worship! These redeemed, special emissaries of God, who are used by God to proclaim the gospel during the Tribulation, are seen pouring out praise to the Lamb—Jesus Christ. Worshiping Jesus Christ is fitting, it is right, it is proper.

So we have every reason, every right, and every command to come *to* the Father, *through* the Son, *in* the Spirit—true trinitarian worship. I don't know about you, but when I think of what the Spirit of God does in my life—bringing me to God, empowering me for service, energizing me for worship—I cannot help but respond to give Him glory, as well as the Father and the Son.

I'm concerned about people who just vaguely worship God. I'm also concerned about people whose worship seems to terminate at the Son—sort of the "Jesus approach." And I also worry about worship that inordinately and incessantly focuses only on the Holy Spirit. *God is to be worshiped in His trinitarian fullness, as the Father of the Lord Jesus Christ, in the energy and power of the blessed Holy Spirit.*

We've talked now about the *importance* of worship, the *source* of worship (our redemption), and the *object* of worship (the Trinity). Let's look at a fourth point:

IV. THE SPHERE (PLACE) OF WORSHIP

In the Old Testament, the people of God clearly worshiped in temples, tabernacles, and very specific geographical locations. This is why the woman of Samaria, in John 4:20, says to Jesus, "Our fathers worshiped in this mountain [Mt. Gerizim]; and ye say that in Jerusalem is the place where men ought to worship." Basically, she was asking Jesus *where* she was supposed to worship. So Jesus answers her in verse 21: "Woman, believe me, the hour cometh, when ye shall neither in this mountain, nor yet at Jerusalem, worship the Father." In other words, Jesus told her that very soon, neither location would be the place of worship because they would both be eliminated.

A. The Symbolism of the Old Covenant

When Jesus told the Samaritan woman that worship would no longer take place on Mount Gerizim or at Jerusalem, He was not denying the significance of the Tabernacle, or the Temple, or the ceremonial and sacrificial systems. He was not denying all the symbols, emblems, and pictures that God had given to His people. He was telling her that the time was coming when all the symbols would pass away and that there wouldn't be a need for a physical Temple, sacrifices, and priests. Why? Because every individual believer would be a living temple and a living priest. Also, the sacrifice that Christ was to offer would be the one, full, final, permanent sacrifice—ending all other sacrifices.

Now there was nothing wrong with the symbols, but they were just that—symbols. God was never limited or confined to the Tabernacle or to the Temple; they were just prodders of the mind—symbols to cause His people to worship. But in the new covenant, the symbols became reality and went from the external to the internal.

Jesus basically told the Samaritan woman that all the locations that were identified as the places of worship would, in just a short time, be eliminated. As you know, when Jesus died, the veil in the Temple was torn from top to bottom, enabling anybody to walk right into the holy of holies (Mark 15:38). And in 70 A.D. the whole Temple was utterly destroyed. The Samaritan temple had already been destroyed in 125 B.C. So the whole system has come to an end.

You say, "Well, if there isn't a Temple, and there isn't a special physical building, where do we worship God?"

B. The Reality of the New Covenant

1. The temple of our individual bodies

In 1 Corinthians 6:19*a*, Paul says, "What? Know ye not that your body is the temple of the Holy Spirit?" As Christians, we are living temples of the Holy Spirit. You say, "Do you mean that I can worship God wherever I go?" That's right! You can worship Him at the beach, in the mountains, in the country, or in your living room; while you're driving down the road, sitting under a tree, walking in the woods, sitting on your porch looking at stars, or smelling the fresh flowers in the morning. You can worship God anywhere you are, under any kind of circumstance or condition, because you are a living, breathing temple in which God dwells. In other words, *the sphere of worship is unlimited.*

You say, "Now does that mean I don't need to go to church?" Well, in one sense, that's true. You don't need to go to church to worship God. But we must look at another dimension:

2. The temple of our collective assembly

There is a place of worship today—a building where God uniquely meets with His people. Let's look at this special building.

a) Ephesians 2:19-22—In Ephesians 2, Paul describes the Christian in some very graphic terms. And he describes them collectively, not as disconnected, individual temples. First, he sees all of us as fellow citizens. "Now, therefore, ye are no more strangers and sojourners, but fellow citizens with the saints" (v. 19*a*). Then he says we all belong to "the household of God" (v. 19*b*). In other words, we're family. Not only are we linked by common citizenship and linked by common blood as family, but verses 20-22 tell us that we are linked together as a building. "And [we] are built upon the foundation of the apostles and prophets, Jesus Christ himself being the chief corner stone, in whom all the building fitly framed together groweth unto an holy temple in the Lord; in whom ye also are built for an habitation of God through the Spirit."

God has a special building. Do you know what it is? It's the visible, living assembly of the redeemed saints. When we come together, we constitute the temple of God in a unique way. So, we are not only individual temples; collectively we are one great temple in which God dwells.

b) 1 Peter 2:5*a*—Peter says, "Ye also, as living stones, are built up a spiritual house." We are "living stones," and when we come together we constitute a place of worship where God manifests Himself in ways unique to the assembly—ways that He cannot be manifested when we are alone—for He moves to us through others.

c) 2 Corinthians 6:16b—Paul says, "For ye are the temple of the living God; as God hath said, I will dwell in them, and walk in them." God moves in our midst when we come together.

d) 1 Corinthians 3:9b, 16-17—At the end of verse 9 Paul says to the Corinthians, "Ye are God's building." Then in verses 16-17 he says, "Know ye not that ye are the temple of God, and that the Spirit of God dwelleth in you? If any man defile the temple of God, him God shall destroy; for the temple of God is holy, which temple ye are."

e) Hebrews 10:24-25a—"And let us consider one another to provoke unto love and to good works, not forsaking the assembling of ourselves together." Why are we to assemble together? Because in a marvelous, unique way we become the living temple of God. We are not a building made with stone, we are a building made with living flesh.

Yes, we can worship God anyplace. We can worship Him all alone in isolation and privacy. But we must also worship God in the assembly of His redeemed people so that we can "stimulate one another to love and good deeds" (Heb. 10:24b, NASB). We can't survive by ourselves. We need the collective assembly—the living stones piled one upon the other that constitute the habitation of the living God.

So worshiping God is not really a geographical issue, but that doesn't mean there's not a special building or a special place of worship. We must come together with God's redeemed people. We don't need special priests or special sacrifices, because we all are living priests, the sacrifice has been offered once for all, and we have immediate access to God on our own. We are His living temple.

When God instituted His worship to take place on the first day of the week, He did it so that we'd be faithful to it. If there's anything in your life that you need to be faithful to, it's the corporate worship on the Lord's Day. You'll not survive out in the world alone. Besides, to neglect the collective assembly of believers is to violate the command of God to not forsake "the assembling of ourselves together" (Heb. 10:25a). The stimulation and affirmation that comes when you're in the presence of God's redeemed people and the unique and wondrous ministry that the Spirit of God accomplishes (which cannot be accomplished in your isolation) are something that you must respond to. Each Lord's Day should find you in the place of worshiping God—with His redeemed people. To forsake that is to put yourself on the outside.

Is your fire going out?

A pastor once went to visit a man who wasn't attending church very faithfully. It was a cold, winter day, so they sat by a fire and warmed themselves as they talked. To this irregular attender the pastor said, "My friend, I don't see you at church on the Lord's Day. You seem to come only when it's convenient or only when you feel like you need to come. You miss so very often—I wish you'd come all the time." The man didn't seem to be getting the message, so the pastor said, "Let me show you something." He then took the tongs from beside the fireplace, pulled open the screen, and began to separate all the coals so that none of them were touching each other. In a matter of moments, the blazing coals had all died out. "My friend," he said, "that is what's happening in your life. As soon as you isolate yourself, the fire goes out."

We're to worship God everywhere, and at all times. But it's also extremely important that we come together in the assembly of His redeemed people to stimulate one another to love and good works and to honor and worship God. I don't like to allow a week to go by in my life when I haven't set aside a special time to worship God with His people—neither should you. Be faithful.

Focusing on the Facts

1. Although God created man to worship Him, what happened instead? What purpose has God sought to accomplish in His redemptive plan (see p. 71)?
2. Explain the balance between ministry and worship. Give an example from the Old Testament (see p. 71).
3. Since we live in the midst of God's spiritual presence (Acts 17:28), when and where is it proper for God to be worshiped (see p. 72)?
4. What was Jesus primarily referring to by designating God as "Father" (John 4:23; see pp. 72-73)?
5. Rather than his submission to or generation from the Father, what was Jesus emphasizing when He used the term "Father"? Therefore, how must God be worshiped (see p. 73)?
6. Cite some Scripture references to show that when Jesus was referring to God as His Father, He was proclaiming His own deity (see pp. 73-74).
7. Why did the Jews seek to kill Jesus in John 5:18 and 10:29-33 (see p. 73)?
8. How can people claim to worship God as the eternal Spirit who is present everywhere and who is their Father and yet not have their worship acceptable to God (see p. 75)?
9. How is God worshiped and identified in the New Testament epistles of Paul, Peter, and John (see pp. 75-76)?
10. How is the honor of the Father and the Son related, according to John 5:23 (see p. 76)?
11. Can we pray to Jesus, or does the Bible teach that we must only pray to the Father? Explain (see p. 76).
12. What did the early church recognize Christ as? How did Thomas address Jesus after the resurrection (John 20:28; see p. 76)?

13. Does Scripture explicitly instruct us to worship the Spirit? What part does the Spirit play in worship? What is His unique ministry in the church age (see p. 77)?

14. Who are the hundred and forty-four thousand emissaries of God seen worshiping in Revelation 14:1-3 (see p. 77)?

15. We have every reason, right, and command to come in worship _____ the Father, _____ the Son, and _____ the Spirit (see p. 78).

16. When Jesus told the Samaritan woman that true worship would no longer take place on Mount Gerizim or at Jerusalem, was He denying the significance of the various elements of the sacrificial system? Explain (see p. 78).

17. Under the New Covenant, why can we worship God anywhere, regardless of what we are doing (1 Cor. 6:19; see p. 79)?

18. In what special building does God uniquely meet with His people today (Eph. 2:19-22; see pp. 79-80)?

19. Besides worshiping God alone, why must we also worship God in the assembly of the redeemed (Heb. 10:24-25; see pp. 80-81)?

Pondering the Principles

1. Many cults say that they believe Jesus Christ is the Son of God, yet they do not acknowledge His deity. The efficacy of Christ's atonement partly rests upon the fact that Christ is God, for no man could atone for the sins of all the men who have ever lived (Ps. 49:7-9). Are you convinced of the deity of Christ? Could you defend His deity to someone who denied it? If your answer is no to either of those questions, you need to study the divine nature of Christ. Examine the explicit claims that are made about and by Him (John 1:1, 14; 8:58; Phil. 2:6); the names that are assumed by Him (compare Joel 2:32 with Rom. 10:13; and Isa. 44:6 with Rev. 1:17); the attributes He possesses that are unique to God (Mic. 5:2; Matt. 28:20; Heb. 13:8); the works He did that only God could do (Mark 2:5-10; Col. 1:15-17); and the worship He received that is appropriate for only God (Matt. 14:33; Luke 24:52; Heb. 1:6).

2. As a Christian, you are a temple of God—He resides within you. Does that fact motivate you to live a life of constant communication with Him? When you experience problems, do you immediately bring them to God, or is He the last to know? When you have been blessed, do you offer a word of thanksgiving on the spot? Cultivate the habit of communicating spiritually with God as naturally as you breathe. Don't wait for a personal quiet time or church service.

3. A believer who lives the Christian life on his own is like an ember that has been separated from other embers in a fire—it will quickly die out unless the heat from the rest of the fire helps to keep it alive. The forces of evil are too powerful, disheartening, and deceitful for a Christian to battle them alone. We need to be spiritually strengthened, emotionally encouraged, and constantly motivated as we face the subtle and overt opposition of the

world's system. Did you know that you are an integral part of the body of Christ and that people at your church should be benefiting from your presence? Make sure that you don't disregard the importance of the mutual ministry that takes place within the context of the church.

7
True Worship—Part 7

Outline

Introduction

Review
I. The Importance of Worship
II. The Source of Worship
II. The Object of Worship
IV. The Sphere of Worship

Lesson
V. The Nature of Worship
   A. The Deviations of Worship in Spirit and Truth
      1. Samaritan Worship (spirit without truth)
      2. Jewish worship (truth without spirit)
   B. The Discussion of Worship in Spirit and Truth
      1. Worship in spirit
         a) The meaning
            (1) Romans 1:9
            (2) Psalm 103:1
            (3) Psalm 51:15-17
         b) The method
            (1) Possession of the Holy Spirit
            (2) Thoughts centered on God
            (3) Discovery and meditation of God's Word
            (4) An undivided heart

Conclusion

Introduction

Years ago, William Temple, the Archbishop of Canterbury, defined worship this way: "To worship is to quicken the conscience by the holiness of God, to feed the mind with the truth of God, to purge the imagination by the beauty of God, to open the heart to the love of God, and to devote the will to the purpose of God." In other words, worship is all that we are responding to all that He is.

Review

I. THE IMPORTANCE OF WORSHIP (see pp. 11-43)

John 4:23 tells us that the Father seeks true worshipers. That makes worship very important. In fact, God saves men to worship Him—making it the goal of God's redemptive plan.

Is the church's focus on God . . . or man?

Evelyn Underhill, writing in 1928 to a conference of Church of England clergy, said, "We are drifting toward a religion which, consciously or unconsciously, keeps its eye on humanity rather than deity."

That's a true statement! Even today, the evangelical church is prone to be man-centered rather than God-centered. We are such a consumptive, pragmatic, man-centered society, that we tend to turn everything on ourselves. We talk of men and their needs, their problems, their programs, their methods, their efforts, their sermons, their songs, their books, their churches, and their organizations. And somehow, in all of that talk, we very often lose sight of the fact that we are to be conscious of God far more than of men.

II. THE SOURCE OF WORSHIP (see pp. 47-51)

In John 4:23, the seeking of the Father is efficacious. In other words, He seeks out individuals to worship Him and then redeems and transforms them into true worshipers. Therefore, the source of worship is salvation.

III. THE OBJECT OF WORSHIP (see pp. 72-78)

When we gather together, it is to focus on God and to worship Him in His trinitarian fullness as Spirit and as the Father of our Lord Jesus Christ. We don't evaluate worship on the basis of what it does for us, asking questions like, "Is is going to meet my needs? Is it going to give me a good feeling? Is it going to inspire me? Is it going to bless me?" To evaluate worship like that is to substitute subjective affection for objective trust. When we gather to worship God, He is the object, and our purpose is to give to Him.

IV. THE SPHERE OF WORSHIP (see pp. 78-81)

In John 4:21 Jesus indicates to the woman of Samaria that the time would come when worship would no longer take place in a specific geographic location. And then in verse 24a, He says, "God is a Spirit." Therefore, we are to worship everywhere. Yet, in our last lesson we saw that there is still a temple where God meets His people. Do you remember what it is? It's the corporate assembly of the living church. Even though we should worship God everywhere at all times, there is still a unique building made up of living stones that are "built together for an habitation of God through the Spirit" (Eph. 2:22b; cf. 1 Pet. 2:5). God is to be worshiped in all places and at all times but also in the corporate assembly of His redeemed people, "not forsaking the assembling of ourselves together" (Heb. 10:25a).

Lesson

V. THE NATURE OF WORSHIP

A. The Deviations of Worship in Spirit and Truth

1. Samaritan worship (spirit without truth)

In John 4:22a, Jesus says to the Samaritan woman, "Ye worship ye know not what." Now, what did He mean by that? Well, He acknowledged that the Samaritans were worshiping, they just didn't know *what* they were worshiping. You see, the Samaritans only accepted the Pentateuch (the first five books of the Old Testament) as coming from God. So their knowledge was limited. They had enough to know some of the truths about God, but not enough to have the full salvation revelation. They were worshiping, but they didn't know the fullness of what they were worshiping.

Samaritan worship, then, was enthusiastic worship without proper information. Their worship was aggressive, enthusiastic, excited, and faithful, but they didn't have the right content. In other words, they worshiped in spirit but not in truth.

Did you know that even though their temple was destroyed in 125 B.C., Samaritan worship is still going on today? There are only about 400 Samaritans still alive, but if you were to go to Mount Gerizim on their holy days, you would see them slicing up animals exactly as it was done during the Mosaic economy. They're still at it, and they will not give it up. They're enthusiastic, but they don't have the right information or content.

2. Jewish worship (truth without spirit)

Back in John 4:22b Jesus says, "We [Jews] know what we worship; for salvation is of the Jews." Now the Jews were just the opposite of the Samaritans. They accepted all thirty-nine books of the Old Testament and had the whole revelation of the teaching of salvation. They had the truth—but they lacked the spirit. Just read Matthew 6:1-8, and you'll see that they were cold, legalistic, and hypocritical. They went through the motions, but their hearts weren't in it. Now I admit that there were some Jews who had a zeal for God, but the basic existing religion of Jerusalem was lifeless. They had the truth, but their hearts were empty.

So, Jerusalem had the truth without the spirit, and Mount Gerizim had the spirit without the truth. Those are the two extreme poles of worship. On the one hand is Mount Gerizim, or enthusiastic heresy. On the other hand is Jerusalem, or barren, lifeless orthodoxy. The Jews had all the accurate data, but they didn't have any heart. The Samaritans had all the heart, but they didn't have the data. What Jesus is saying is that both spirit and truth must be present in true worship. One without the other causes an imbalance. Sincere, enthusiastic, aggressive worship is great, but it must be based on truth.

Worship based on truth is essential, but if it doesn't issue in an eager, anxious, thrilled heart, it's lacking. Often we can have light without heat or heat without light, but true worship demands a balance.

B. The Discussion of Worship in Spirit and Truth

In John 4:23a, Jesus says, "But the hour cometh, and now is, when the true worshipers shall worship the Father in spirit and in truth." And then in verse 24b, He says, "They that worship him must worship him in spirit and in truth." Let's look at these two elements of true worship:

1. Worship in spirit

   a) The meaning

   Worshiping in spirit refers to the human spirit—the inner person. We are to worship from the inside out. It's not a matter of being in the right place at the right time, with the right words, the right demeanor, the right clothes, the right formalities, the right activities, the right music, or the right mood. No! It is what's on the inside—the spirit.

   (1) Romans 1:9—Paul says, "For God is my witness, whom I serve [Gk., *latreuō*, 'worship'] with my spirit." Paul worshiped God with his spirit.

   (2) Psalm 103:1—David writes, "Bless the Lord, O my soul, and all that is within me, bless his holy name." David is talking here about glorifying God from within.

   (3) Psalm 51:15-17—David comes to God with the worship of repentance and says, "O Lord, open thou my lips, and my mouth shall show forth thy praise. For thou desirest not sacrifice, else would I give it; thou delightest not in burnt offering. The sacrifices of God are a broken spirit; a broken and contrite heart, O God, thou wilt not despise."

   David acknowledged that God wasn't interested in the external sacrifices, because they were just symbols of what God really wanted—the heart. And when he said, "Open thou my lips, and my mouth shall show forth thy praise," do you know what that says to me? That pictures a man whose heart is filled with praise, but because of his circumstances and a lack of strength, he needs God to open his mouth so that the praise will come pouring out. That's what it means to worship in spirit.

   b) The method

   How can we worship in spirit? How can we be so filled with praise that when our mouths are pried open it just gushes out? How can we keep from having cold hearts—bored and indifferent? Let me give you several principles on how to worship in spirit.

(1) Possession of the Holy Spirit

Before we can worship God in our spirits, the Holy Spirit must be there to prompt worship. According to 1 Corinthians 2:11*b*, "Even so the things of God knoweth no man, but the Spirit of God." So if you don't have the Spirit of God within you, prompting your heart, motivating your heart, cleansing your heart, and instructing your heart—worship isn't going to happen. God cannot be worshiped without His Spirit energizing that worship. That's basic. That's the bottom line.

You have to be saved to worship God. Once you're saved, the Holy Spirit comes to live in your heart to point you to God, to prod you, to poke you, to push you, to instruct you, and to purge you so that you can worship. That's His ministry. It all begins with the resident Holy Spirit. We worship God in our human spirit because we are prompted by the Holy Spirit to do so.

In 1 Corinthians 12:3*b* it says, "No man can say that Jesus is the Lord, but by the Holy Spirit." In other words, a person can't affirm the lordship of Christ or worship Him as sovereign unless the Holy Spirit prods him. So worship begins with the Spirit of God.

(2) Thoughts centered on God

Worship is an overflow of a mind renewed by the truth of God. Contemplating God is the trigger that sets off worship. Now contemplating God, or thinking thoughts about Him, can be translated into the familiar word *meditation*. True worship comes forth out of meditation. You say, "Well, what exactly is meditation?" *To meditate is to focus your whole mind on one subject.*

If you find it hard to focus your whole mind on one subject, it's fairly normal—especially in our distracting world. We are exposed to so many things through the media that our minds are cluttered, and our attention spans are very limited. But let me tell you something—the key to effective worship is to be able to concentrate your whole mind on one subject, to meditate on God.

(3) Discovery and meditation on God's Word

Meditation is based on information. If you're going to be thinking on one subject, you have to have a subject to think on. That's basic! The best, the purest, the truest, the most wonderful and blessed meditation is based on what I like to call *discovery*. In other words, when you discover a great truth about God, begin to meditate on that truth until it captivates every element of your whole thinking process. That meditation will give rise to worship.

You say, "Well, if worship is based on meditation, and meditation is based on discovery, what is discovery based on?" Discovery is based on time spent with God in prayer and in the Word. Sadly, we primarily see prayer as a way to get things, and we have lost sight of its communion element—living in the consciousness of God's wonderful presence and just communing with Him there.

Do you get bored in church?

If you get bored in church, may I suggest to you that it's not a commentary on the sermon—it's a commentary on your heart! Even if the sermon isn't particularly worth listening to, the chance to pick up some truths about God that come through, and then to meditate on them, should be the most exhilarating time of your life. If you're uninterested or indifferent, it's not a commentary on the sermon, it's a commentary on you.

You see, if you go to church thinking, "I hope the preacher's got something to say that will get me into a worship mood," you've missed it. By the time Sunday rolls around, you should be so eager to worship with the assembly of believers that you can hardly wait to get into the place to get started. Why? Because you should be in the process of meditating over what you discovered in the Word of God throughout the week. As you study the Word of God, commune with him in prayer, discover truths about Him, and meditate on those truths, the joy of worship will appear.

C. H. Spurgeon said, "Why is it that some people are often in a place of worship and yet they are not holy. . . ? It is because they neglect their [prayer] closets. They love the wheat, but they do not grind it; they would have the corn, but they will not go forth into the fields to gather it; the fruit hangs upon the tree, but they will not pluck it; the water flows at their feet, but they will not stoop to drink of it." Worship isn't passive—it takes effort!

We've been rooted and grounded in Christ, but how deep our roots grow and how beautiful our fruit appears depends, to a large degree, on our process of discovery and meditation on God's wonderful truth. Now I know it's hard for us to meditate. It's difficult for us to isolate our minds on one subject. But it's a discipline—we have to train ourselves to be able to do it. I think about those men who learn how to sit in the middle of the teeming mass of humanity in India and contemplate their navels for days at a time in an undistracted fashion, and I wonder why Christians can't think on God without being distracted.

Worship in the spirit, then, begins with the resident Holy Spirit. Second, our thoughts must be centered on God. Third, we must be involved in discovery and meditation, which arise out of time spent in prayer and Bible study. May I make it simple? No discovery—no meditation; no meditation—no worship. If you go to church with a heart filled with discovery from your own study (or even if you've learned it from somebody else) and you've meditated on it and made it your own, you're going to find that when your mouth is pried open it will overflow with praise.

A fourth principle for worshiping in spirit is:

(4) An undivided heart

In Psalm 86: 5-10 we see David worshiping and glorifying God for who He is and for what He's done. "For Thou, Lord, art good, and ready to forgive, and plenteous in mercy unto all those who call upon thee. Give ear, O Lord, unto my prayer, and attend to the voice of my supplications. In the day of my trouble I will call upon thee; for thou wilt answer me. Among the gods there is none like unto thee, O Lord; neither are there any works like unto thy works. All nations whom thou has made shall come and worship before thee, O Lord, and shall glorify thy name. For thou art great, and doest wondrous things; thou art God alone."

David was pouring out his heart to God—extolling His wonders and His virtues. But his worship was hindered in two areas—he was lacking the truth and he was lacking an undivided heart. Look at verse 11. "Teach me thy way, O Lord; I will walk in thy truth; unite my heart to fear thy name."

First of all, David was lacking the thrill of discovery. Now, sometimes discovery isn't discovering something you didn't previously know; it can also refer to discovering something you knew before, and forgot—or discovering something you knew before and remembered, but never saw with such clarity. So, David asked the Lord to help him in his discovery process.

I would just like to suggest that when you find it difficult to worship, to meditate on God's Word, to go through the process of discovery, or to let God touch your life with his Word to produce praise, you need to stop and ask the Holy Spirit to be your teacher. He is the one who teaches us all things (1 John 2:27; cf. John 16:13).

Second, at the end of verse 11, David says, "Unite my heart to fear thy name." The phrase "fear thy name" was a euphemism for worship. In other words, David wanted to worship God, but he needed to have his heart united. What's the opposite of a united heart? A divided heart. The first problem David had in worshiping God was that he didn't have the truth he needed to meditate on. But second, he was distracted—he had a divided heart.

90

We've all experienced a divided heart, haven't we? Times where we sit down and say, "I'm going to pray now and spend some time with the Lord." But no sooner do we get started than our minds begin to flood with all sorts of distractions, or the kids come blasting through the door at the moment of our greatest discovery! It's so difficult for us to concentrate, and I imagine it was even more difficult for David. After all, he was a king, and he had a lot on his mind. Not only was he concerned about all that was going on in his kingdom, but there were many things in his personal life that weren't right. So he basically said, "God, I want to worship You; but I need an undivided heart to go along with the right instruction. I want to discover, and I want to be able to meditate without being distracted."

Conclusion

When you try to focus your spirit on worship, there will be one major hindrance—self. When you get in front of God, your worship will be hindered. You see, we often have things that we want to do to fulfill our own desires, so we don't have time for discovery, or prayer, or meditation, or worship. And it's hard to have an undivided heart because we're always thinking about our projects, or our activities, or our needs. Self always gets in the way of worship. And we can't really be free to worship God until we eliminate self altogether and become lost in worshiping God. It really comes down to the fact that we are just too lazy to make the effort. We're so self-indulgent with ease that we won't expend ourselves to dig deep, to scoop up the water, to pluck the grain, as Spurgeon said.

One of the great experiences of my brief life has been to read Stephen Charnock's book *The Existence and Attributes of God*. It contains all of his thoughts about God—rich, profound insights—and takes an entire lifetime to digest. At one point, he says this; "To pretend homage to God and intend only the advantage to myself is rather to mock God than to worship Him. When we believe we ought to be satisfied rather than God glorified, we set God below ourselves and imagine that He should submit His own honor to our advantage." That's the hindrance to worship—when we set ourselves and our needs, advantages, blessings, and so on, above God.

Let's be free to worship God. When we come together in the assembly of His redeemed people, may our lives be so filled with praise from time spent with God in prayer, study, discovery, and meditation, that when our mouths are opened, praise might burst forth and our inner spirit offer true worship to Him.

Focusing on the Facts

1. What was the nature of Samaritan worship? Why was it limited (see p. 86)?

2. In contrast to Samaritan worship, what was the general nature of Jewish worship? What did the Jews lack (see p. 86)?

3. The two extreme poles of worship are enthusiastic _____ and lifeless _____ (see p. 86).

4. What two ingredients did Jesus say must be present in true worship for there to be a proper balance (John 4:23-24; see p. 87)?

5. What does it mean to worship in the spirit (see p. 87)?

6. According to Psalm 51:15-17, what was God not interested in? Why (see p. 87)?

7. What must a Christian have to prompt him to worship (1 Cor. 12:3; see p. 88)?

8. Define meditation as it relates to worship. Why is it difficult today for Christians to meditate (see p. 88)?

9. How can the discovery of a great truth result in worship? What are the sources of discovering spiritual truth (see pp. 88-89)?

10. Explain the wrong perspective of prayer that many Christians have (see p. 88).

11. If you get bored in church, what is the primary problem? Explain (see p. 89).

12. Does the process of discovering spiritual truths refer only to discovering something new? Explain (see p. 90).

13. Who should be our teacher in the practice of meditation? Why (John 16:13; see p. 90)?

14. Why did David pray for God to unite his heart (Ps. 86:11; see p. 90)?

15. What can be a major hindrance when you try to focus your spirit on worship? Explain (see p. 91).

Pondering the Principles

1. How would you rate the nature of your worship? Is it more like Samaritan worship or Jewish worship? If you are weak in the area of truth, increase the time you spend in your personal study of God's Word through tapes, books, or classes about the Bible. If you feel you are gifted as a teacher, begin leading a Bible study for those who are not as spiritually mature as you. Nothing forces you to learn better and faster than having to prepare to communicate to others what you have learned. If you are weak in the area of enthusiasm, listen to or read the testimonies of how God has worked mightily in the lives of others. Recognizing that God is actively involved in the business of transforming lives can give you a renewed sense of vitality. Or associate regularly with committed Christians who are excited about their ministries. Imagine what effect a dynamo like Paul had on a young, timid man like Timothy.

2. Have you ever found yourself justifying not going to church or not paying attention to the message because you've heard it before? Some key elements in the process of spiritual growth are remembrance and repetition. Peter expressed the importance of them: "So I will always remind you of these things, even though you know them and are firmly established in the truth you now have. I think it is right to refresh your memory as long as I live. And I will make every effort to see that after my departure you will

always be able to remember these things" (2 Pet. 1:12-13, 15; NIV*). Don't ever think that you have grasped all the important truths contained in the Bible. If you remain teachable, you will gain new and deeper insights to the truths you thought you had once mastered.

3. Paul emphasized the necessity of meditating on God's Word when he said, "Let the word of Christ dwell in you richly as you teach and admonish one another" (Col. 3:16, NIV; cf. Phil. 4:8-9). Do you take time to reflect upon the Scripture you read? Or, do you race through the Bible so that you can stay on your Bible-reading schedule? Reading the Bible is of little value unless you make time to ponder the spiritual truths you find and allow the Spirit to implant them in your heart. As you read, put question marks by the verses you don't understand. Begin a systematic study of those problem spots. If a passage is unclear, reread it. Put a key verse on a card and memorize it, or meditate on it as you work around the house or drive your car. Follow the example of the psalmist, who meditated on the Word "day and night" and became well nourished and fruitful (Ps. 1:2-3).

*New International Version.

8

True Worship—Part 8

Outline

Introduction

Review
I. The Importance of Worship
II. The Source of Worship
III. The Object of Worship
IV. The Sphere of Worship
V. The Nature of Worship
   A. The Deviations of Worship in Spirit and Truth
   B. The Discussion of Worship in Spirit and Truth
     1. Worship in spirit
       a) The meaning
       b) The method
         (1) Possession of the Holy Spirit
         (2) Thoughts centered on God
         (3) Discovery and meditation on God's Word
         (4) An undivided heart

Lesson
         (*a*) Psalm 86:5-11
         (*b*) Psalm 108:1-3
         (*c*) Psalm 112:7*b*-8*a*
         (*d*) Psalm 57:7-11
         (5) An open and repentant spirit
     2. Worship in truth
       a) Romans 1:18-19, 25
       b) Psalm 47:7*b*
       c) 2 Corinthians 4:2
       d) Acts 2:42*a*
       e) 1 Timothy 4:13
       f) Colossians 3:16-17
       g) Acts 17:23
VI. The Results of Worship
   A. God Is Glorified
   B. Christians Are Purified

C. The Church Is Edified
D. The Lost Are Evangelized
VII. The Preparation for Worship (Heb. 10:22)
  A. The Call
  B. The Checkpoints
    1. Sincerity
    2. Fidelity
    3. Humility
    4. Purity
VIII. The Barriers of Worship
  A. The Worship of Repentance
  B. The Worship of Acceptance
  C. The Worship of Devotion

Introduction

Recently, I have been greatly concerned about the matter of worship. Wondering whether this concern was unique to my own era, I began reading the works of some of the more ancient scriptural commentators and saints of God. What I found out was that they faced similar periods of time when the church had lost its perspective on worship. In fact, throughout church history there seemed to be a rather constant cry, calling the people of God to a worshiping life. For example, St. Anselm of Canterbury (1033-1109) said this: "Up, slight man. Flee for a little while thy occupations. Hide thyself for a time from thy disturbing thoughts. Pass away now thy toilsome cares, and put away thy burdensome business. Yield room for some little time with God and rest for a little time in Him, and through the inner chamber shut out all thoughts save those of God and such as can aid thee in seeking Him. . . . Speak now to God saying, 'I seek Thy face. Thy face, Lord, will I seek.' " And thus did he call his people to worship.

Review

In our look at worship, we've tried not to exhaust the theme, but rather to just touch the edges of it so that the Spirit of God might begin to teach us. So far, we've looked at a definition of worship (see p. 8) and discussed:

I. THE IMPORTANCE OF WORSHIP (see pp. 11-43)

II. THE SOURCE OF WORSHIP (see pp. 47-51)

III. THE OBJECT OF WORSHIP (see pp. 72-78)

IV. THE SPHERE OF WORSHIP (see pp. 78-81)

In our last lesson we began a look at:

V. THE NATURE OF WORSHIP (begins on p. 86)

  A. The Deviations of Worship in Spirit and Truth

  B. The Discussion of Worship in Spirit and Truth

    1. Worship in spirit

a) The meaning

b) The method

    (1) Possession of the Holy Spirit

    (2) Thoughts centered on God

    (3) Discovery and meditation on God's Word

    (4) An undivided heart

Many times in the Old Testament, God indicted His people for worshiping Him externally while their hearts were far from Him (Isa. 29:13; Jer. 3:10; Ezek. 33:31). In fact, the Lord indicted the religious people of His day for the same thing. For example, in Matthew 15:7-9*a* He says, "Ye hypocrites, well did Isaiah prophesy of you, saying, This people draweth near unto me with their mouth, and honoreth me with their lips, but their heart is far from me. But in vain they do worship me." You see, God desires an undivided heart.

Lesson

Now we'll pick up where we left off.

    (*a*) Psalm 86:5-11 (see pp. 90-91).

    (*b*) Psalm 108:1-3—"O God, my heart is fixed; I will sing and give praise. . . . Awake, psaltery and harp; I myself will awake early. I will praise thee, O Lord, among the peoples; and I will sing praises unto thee among the nations." In other words, the music of praise rises out of a fixed, undivided, settled heart—a heart focusing only on God.

    (*c*) Psalm 112:7*b*-8*a*—This psalm starts out, "Praise ye the Lord," and then continues as a psalm of praise. How is it that the psalmist's heart can praise? Because "his heart is fixed, trusting in the Lord" (v. 7*b*) and because "his heart is established" (v. 8*a*). Praise, then, arises out of a heart that is fixed, established, and focused on the wonder of God.

    (*d*) Psalm 57:7-11—"My heart is fixed, O God, my heart is fixed; I will sing and give praise. Awake up, my glory; awake, psaltery and harp. I myself will awake early. I will praise thee, O Lord, among the peoples; I will sing unto thee among the nations. For thy mercy is great unto the heavens, and thy truth unto the clouds. Be thou exalted, O God, above the heavens; let thy glory be above all the earth."

So to worship in spirit we must possess the Holy Spirit, our thoughts must be centered on God, we must be in the

Word of God with discovery and meditation, and then we must also have an undivided and fixed heart. Fifth, we must have:

(5) An open and repentant spirit

In Psalm 139:23-24 David says, "Search me, O God, and know my heart; try me, and know my thoughts; and see if there be any wicked way in me, and lead me in the way everlasting." David was admitting here that he couldn't fully understand his own heart. So he asked God to show him anything in his life that he needed to repent of.

As we approach God in worship, we need to come with an open and repentant spirit. We must come to God with a willingness to say, "God, turn on the searchlight and expose whatever You find in the corners." If you have found it difficult to worship, and there's little sense of the nearness of God, it may well be that there are areas in your life that you have long overlooked and are only known about by God. If that's the case, you need to plead with Him to search those areas out and expose them to you. Then you need to willingly confess them in a broken and contrite spirit.

In order to worship, our sins must be dealt with. When Scripture talks about worship, it also talks about cleansing, purging, purifying, confessing, and repenting. Why? Because the only person who can utterly enter into communion with an utterly holy God, is one whose sin is utterly dealt with. *We can't go rushing into God's presence in our impurity, thinking that all is well!* We, like Isaiah, must confess our sin before God and allow Him to touch that live, burning coal to our lips to purge us (Isa. 6:6-7).

When the Spirit of God resides within us, when our minds are focused on God, when we're in His Word discovering and meditating with an undivided heart, and when we have given God full access to uncover whatever stands between us and Him—that is worshiping in spirit.

Many years ago, Stephen Charnock wrote these words: "Without the heart it is not worship; it is a stage play; an acting a part without being that person really . . . a hypocrite. . . . We may truly be said to worship God—though we lack perfection; but we cannot be said to worship Him if we lack sincerity. . . ." That's so true! *We may worship imperfectly, but we cannot worship insincerely.* When we come to God to worship in spirit, it must be from the depth of all that is within us—a sincere worship of God.

Now, let's look at the second (and balancing) element of the nature of worship.

2. Worship in truth

All worship is in response to truth. It is not an emotional exercise with "God words" and induced feelings, it is a response that is built upon truth.

Pilate asked Jesus a very important question: "What is *truth?*" (John 18:38*a*). Well, the answer to his question is found in John 17:17*b*, where Jesus says to His Father, "Thy word is truth," or in Psalm 119 where the psalmist says, "Thy law is the truth" (v. 142*b*), "Thy word is true" (v. 160*a*).

Now, if we are to worship in truth, and the Word of God is truth, then we must worship out of an understanding of the Word of God. If we're going to truly worship God, we must understand who He is, and the only place He has fully revealed Himself is in His Word.

a) Romans 1:18-19, 25

"For the wrath of God is revealed from heaven against all ungodliness and unrighteousness of men, who hold the truth in unrighteousness, because that which may be known of God is manifest in them; for God hath shown it unto them." God has disclosed Himself, first of all, in terms of conscience and creation, or what is called general revelation. But men suppressed that truth and "exchanged the truth of God for a lie, and worshiped and served the creature more than the Creator" (v. 25).

First of all, God revealed Himself in creation and conscience, and then He revealed Himself clearly in the pages of the Word of God. *If we are to worship in truth, then we are to worship God as He is defined in the Bible,* because only the Bible explains the God of creation and conscience. Everything we know about God is in the Word of God, so He can't be worshiped apart from His revelation.

b) Psalm 47:7*b*

All worship must be based on truth. This is seen in Psalm 47:7*b*, where the Psalmist says, "Sing ye praises with understanding." Worship is not simply holding hands and swaying back and forth or having ecstatic experiences that have no meaning or content. Worship is not even a good feeling, as good as feelings are. Worship is an expression of praise from the depth of the heart toward a God who is understood through His Word. *There's no virtue in saying you're worshiping God if you don't comprehend what you're doing.* Why? Because there's no true worship apart from a true understanding of God. Any group that does not understand truth about God does not worship God—cannot worship God—for He must be worshiped in spirit and according to truth.

c) 2 Corinthians 4:2

Paul says, "But [we] have renounced the hidden things of dishonesty, not walking in craftiness, nor handling the word of God deceitfully, but by manifestation of the truth commending ourselves to every man's conscience in the sight of God." In other words, Paul says, "We will never deceitfully misuse the Bible, nor will we ever be dishonest with anybody to gain our own ends. All we desire to do is to manifest the truth and to therefore commend ourselves in the sight of God." All response in worship is a response to the Word of God.

Why is expository preaching important?

People often ask me, "How can you have a worship service when you preach such a long time? When do the people have time to worship?" Well, I'm so committed to expository preaching because God cannot be worshiped apart from an understanding of who He is as He is revealed in Scripture. I'm committed to the systematic teaching of the Word of God—week in and week out—because God must be worshiped in truth. Now I could give clever sermons that would move the emotions and the attitudes by filling them with a lot of stories. And I could make it all very interesting, fun, and exciting. However, when it was all said and done people might say, "Boy, John MacArthur can sure preach!" but they wouldn't be worshiping God. It's a far greater challenge for me to teach the Word of God and let it command men to respond to God as God is revealed in His self-revelation.

I strongly believe that any young person going into the ministry who is not committed to expository preaching is ultimately cutting his own throat. Why? Because people must respond, in every dimension of their lives, to the truth of the Word of God. We have to worship in truth—truth that is revealed in His Word. That's why I'm so totally committed to the fact that we must teach the Word of God.

d) Acts 2:42a

When the early church met together, they "continued steadfastly in the apostles' doctrine." What was their doctrine? The revelations of God about Himself that were manifested through the apostles' writings and teachings. They were the substance of the truth on which the early church worshiped.

e) 1 Timothy 4:13

Paul told Timothy, "Till I come, give attendance to reading, to exhortation, to doctrine." In other words, "Read the text, explain the text, and apply the text." Timothy was to stay in the text and teach sound doctrine—the truth about God.

f) Colossians 3:16-17

When the early church worshiped, they used "psalms and hymns and spiritual songs" and had times of praise and thanks. But before all these things are listed in verses 16-17, it says, "Let the word of Christ dwell in you richly [Gk., *plousiōs*, "abundantly, fully"]." In other words, when the Word

99

dominates us, our praise is regulated, and our worship is conformed to the divine standard.

g) Acts 17:23

When Paul went to Mars Hill in Athens, he saw the people worshiping—but their worship was unacceptable. Look at his indictment of them: "For as I passed by, and beheld your devotions, I found an altar with this inscription, TO THE UNKNOWN GOD. Whom, therefore, ye ignorantly worship. . . ." You see, they were worshiping in ignorance, and their worship was unacceptable.

So what is the nature of worship? It's offering God worship from the depths of our inner being in praise, prayer, song, giving, and living—but always based on His revealed truth. It's difficult to keep the church conformed to that because on one hand it tends to get cold and lifeless, but on the other hand it gets emotional, fanatical, and feeling-oriented. The balance is in the middle because God is to be worshiped in spirit *and* in truth.

A loss of true worship is seen in cold orthodoxy where ritual, formality, routine, and tradition have become a mindless, meaningless activity—that is just as much a loss as the ecstasies of the other extreme. So I submit to you, if you're going to worship God, there must be faithful commitment to the Word of God. It isn't going to happen by some "zap" out of heaven. Worship must come from the overflow of an understanding of God's Word. As you study it, discover its truths, meditate on it, focus on God, have an undivided heart, and have an open and repentant spirit—the result will be an overflow of worship.

VI. THE RESULTS OF WORSHIP

A. God Is Glorified

Psalm 50:23a says, "Whoso offereth praise glorifieth me." When we praise and worship God, He is glorified. In Leviticus 10:3b, the Lord tells Moses, "I will be sanctified in them that come near me, and before all the people I will be glorified." God wants to be set apart and glorified among His people. And as we come to Him in worship, He is glorified. The supreme purpose of life is to glorify God—and when we worship Him as He is to be worshiped, He is glorified.

Second, when we worship God as He desires to be worshiped:

B. Christians Are Purified

In Psalm 24:3-4 David says, "Who shall ascend into the hill of the Lord? Or who shall stand in his holy place? He who hath clean hands, and a pure heart." A worshiping church is a pure church. Why? Because as we enter into God's presence there is a recognition of our sinfulness and a willingness to abandon that sinfulness. There is a consuming desire to be pure and clean, the closer we draw to God. And the nearer we come to Him, the more overwhelmed we become with our sinfulness and cry with David, "Search me, O God, and know

100

my heart; try me, and know my thoughts; and see if there be any wicked way in me" (Ps. 139:23-24a).

The reason the Lord's Table is so important in the worship of the church is because it causes us to regularly face the reality of our sinfulness. In fact, that's the reason the early church so frequently engaged in it—so that they might come face to face with the need to be pure.

Where true worship occurs, not only is God glorified and Christians purified, but third:

C. The Church Is Edified

In Acts 2:47 we read that when the early church was worshiping, they not only found favor with God, but they also found favor with all the people. Then it says, "And the Lord added to the church daily such as should be saved." They filled the city with their doctrine (Acts 5:28b) and turned the world upside down. They were winsome, attractive, and dynamic.

I believe that a worshiping church is a church that is built up—edified. Now I'm not talking about people *feeling* better; I'm talking about people *living* better and becoming transformed. As we come together to worship the Lord, we become built up, strong, and transformed.

Let me say that another way—*True worship changes people.* If you're not changed after you worship, you haven't been worshiping. No one can draw nigh into the presence of God without changing—it can't be done! If worship doesn't propel you into greater obedience, call it what you will, but it isn't worship. It isn't worship unless you come out of it with a greater commitment to obedience. As worship begins in holy expectancy, it ends in holy expentancy—or it isn't worship.

The results of worship are that God is glorified, Christians are purified, the church is edified, and fourth:

D. The Lost Are Evangelized

The profound testimony of a worshiping community probably has a greater impact that any single sermon does. In 1 Corinthians 14:23-25 Paul basically says to the Corinthian church, "If you'll just get your worship shaped up and do it the way it ought to be done, the unbelievers that come into your midst will fall on their faces and worship God." *Worshiping people have a great impact on the lost.*

I'll never forget the Jewish lady who went to the temple down the street from our church to get counsel for her marriage, which was breaking up. She hadn't paid her temple dues, so they wouldn't counsel her. Well, it happened to be on a Sunday, and as she left the temple, she got caught in the crowd coming to church and wound up in the worship service. I baptized her a few weeks later, and she said to me, "I don't remember anything you said that morning. In fact, I couldn't even tell you what the sermon was about. But I was in awe of the joy, the peace, and the love that was going on among the people of the congregation as they worshiped. I had never seen anything like it before." As a result of seeing worshiping people, she became a Christian.

So the results of worship are that God is glorified, Christians are purified, the church is edified, and the lost are evangelized.

Now, some of you are saying to yourself, "John, I understand that the *importance* of worship is that God seeks worshipers; I understand that the *source* of worship is my salvation; I understand that the *object* of worship is God; I understand that the *sphere* of worship is everywhere at all times, especially in the corporate assembly of redeemed people; I understand that the *essence* or *nature* of worship is that it must be perfectly balanced between spirit and truth—the heart and the Word of God; and I understand the *results* of worship. What do I do now? How do I really prepare myself to worship?"

VII. THE PREPARATION FOR WORSHIP (Heb. 10:22)

When you go to church to worship, the issue is not how well prepared the choir or the preacher is. The issue is, How well prepared are *you* to worship God? I believe that one verse, Hebrews 10:22, is the greatest summation of the preparation for worship anywhere in the Bible: "Let us draw near with a true heart in full assurance of faith, having our hearts sprinkled from an evil conscience, and our bodies washed with pure water."

A. The Call

"Let us draw near."

This is a call to worship. Who are we to draw near to? God. The writer of Hebrews is saying, "Come on, it's time to worship. Let's draw near and move toward God."

You say, "That's what I want to do, I want to draw near. But what do I do now?" Well, there are four checkpoints:

B. The Checkpoints

1. Sincerity—"with a true heart"

   Are you really sincere? Is your heart fixed and undivided? Are you worshiping with your whole heart?

2. Fidelity—"in full assurance of faith"

   The Hebrews, to whom this Epistle is addressed, were still trying to hold on to the old covenant. But because the new covenant had come in Jesus Christ, they had to say no to the old covenant in order to worship God. There were no more ceremonies, sacrifices, symbols, pictures, or types. The old was gone, and a new and better covenant had come. So they had to be willing to say, "I'm coming to God in full confidence and assurance that I am no longer under a system of works or ceremony but that I come fully by faith in Jesus Christ." That's fidelity.

   So, not only are you to worship with sincerity, but you are to worship according to the truth as revealed in the New Testament, in full assurance that it is saving truth. You're not to hang on to any of your own works, any of your own worthiness, any of your self-righteousness, or any of your rituals. You're to be fully assured that you can come to God simply and only through faith.

3. Humility—"having our hearts sprinkled from an evil conscience"

We must come to God with the knowledge that we're unworthy to be in His presence because our hearts are filled with an evil conscience. We must also realize that the only reason we can come to God is because we've been sprinkled by the blood of Jesus Christ, which was shed for us on the cross to take care of our sin and cleanse our evil hearts. So as we worship, there's a sense of humility and unworthiness—knowing that we have no business being in the presence of God, except for the fact that the Lord has sprinkled us clean from the evil that is in us.

So to worship God you must pass the test of sincerity, fidelity, humility, and fourth:

4. Purity—"and our bodies washed with pure water"

This is not the same as the cleansing of our hearts at the cross, this is the daily washing. Before we can worship, we have to deal with the sin in our lives through confession. Even though our hearts were cleansed at the cross, our feet still pick up the dust of the world. So there must be a confessing of sin.

Every time you worship, prepare yourself by asking these questions: Am I sincere? Is my heart fixed? Is my whole heart devoted to God? Am I focusing on Him? Am I seeing Him in the Word, through discovery and meditation, so that my hungering desire is to draw nigh unto Him? Am I assured that I can come simply and only by faith, having the full assurance that it is sufficient? Am I coming to God with the knowledge that the only reason I am here is because of what Christ has done for me? And am I coming in purity—having dealt with any sin in my life?

I dare say that if you would just take a little extra time on Sunday mornings to open your Bible to Hebrews 10:22 and go through the checkpoints, you would do more to prepare your heart for worship than any other thing I know.

Are you sincere? Are you committed to the truth of the new covenant? Are you placing all of the rights to your access to God on the finished work of Christ? And are you pure—having dealt with the sin in your life? If you are, you can "Draw nigh to God, and he will draw nigh to you" (James 4:8a).

Some of you have been attending church for years, but you've never really drawn nigh unto God, nor have you ever sensed His nearness—even in your own private devotion and prayer. If that's the case, your worship is probably being hindered.

VIII. THE BARRIERS OF WORSHIP

A. The Worship of Repentance

If there is sin in your life, you have to accept the responsibility for it and confess it. In 2 Samuel 12 we find David after he had committed adultery with Bathsheba, after he had had her husband murdered, and after he had seen the child born of that union die. After all of that, verse 20a says, "Then David arose from the earth, and washed, and anointed himself, and changed his apparel, and came into the house of the Lord, and worshiped." That is the worship of repentance.

You say, "What do you mean by that?" Well, David was in the midst of a tragic situation—the loss of his baby son—and yet he worshiped God. Why? Because he knew he was receiving what he deserved. In the midst of his chastening he worshiped. The worship of repentance means that even in the midst of chastening, you are able to pour out your heart to God, confess your sin, and say, "I'm getting what I deserve."

Some of you can't worship because you've never dealt with your sin and poured out you heart in repentance to God. You may even be angry or bitter over some of the things you've been chastened by. If that's the situation with you, the barrier you have to first overcome is repentance over your sin.

B. The Worship of Acceptance

In the familiar words of Job, when he heard the news that everything he loved was gone—his children, his possessions, his animals—the Bible says, "Then Job arose, and tore his mantle, and shaved his head, and fell down upon the ground, and worshiped, and said, Naked came I out of my mother's womb, and naked shall I return there. The Lord gave, and the Lord hath taken away; blessed be the name of the Lord" (Job 1:20-21). That is the worship of an unquestionable acceptance.

Some of you have never been able to worship God because you're still unable to accept some of the circumstances God has brought into your life. They've made you bitter, and you can't worship. And until you get to the point of acceptance, you're never going to be able to worship God.

George Mueller put it like this: "There came a day when I died; died to the praise and the criticism of men; died to everything except the will of God for my life." And may I suggest, that was the day he began to live? Job also said, "But he knoweth the way that I take; when he hath tested me, I shall come forth as gold" (Job 23:10).

The worship of acceptance is to be willing to accept your circumstances—your place in life, your job, your career, your partner, your children—and be willing to say, "God, You know all of the things that are happening to me (the loss of your loved one, the loss of your child, the loss of your job, the pain of illness), and yet in the midst of it all, I will worship You."

You see, sin, as well as bitterness and an inability to accept what God has brought into your life, will keep you from worshiping.

C. The Worship of Devotion

In Genesis 22, Abraham took his son Isaac to Mount Moriah because God had told him to slay Isaac and offer him as a burnt offering (v. 2). Look what it says in verses 4-5:"Then on the third day Abraham lifted up his eyes, and saw the place afar off. And Abraham said unto his young men, Abide ye here with the ass; and I and the lad will go yonder and worship, and come again to you." The fact that Abraham was willing to take the life of his own son and still see it as worship is incredible. You see, that's devoting oneself to worship, no matter what the cost. Some people can't worship God because they can't bother to get out of bed! How far is that from being willing to stick a knife in the chest of your own beloved son because that's what God told you to do?

Some people can't be free to worship until they overcome some barriers. Either they're not willing to deal with their sin, or they're not willing to deal with their circumstances, or they're not willing to pay the price.

Are we losing our "Oh!"?

A. W. Tozer said this: "Are we losing our 'Oh!'? . . . When the heart on its knees moves into the awesome presence, and hears with fear and wonder things not lawful to utter, the mind falls flat, and words, previously its faithful servants, become weak and totally incapable of telling what the heart hears and sees. In that awful moment, the worshiper can only cry 'Oh!' "

Are we losing our "Oh!"? I pray not!

Focusing on the Facts

1. How did the hypocritical Jewish leaders worship, according to the prophetic indictment spoken by Jesus in Matthew 15:7-9? What type of heart did they lack (see p. 96)?

2. Why did David ask God to search his heart in Psalm 139:23-24 (see p. 97)?

3. What is one thing we should do if we lack a sense of nearness to God? Why (Isa. 6:6-7; cf. Ps. 66:18; see p. 97)?

4. We may worship God _____, but we can't worship Him _____ (see p. 97).

5. Is worship purely an emotional response? What must it be based on an understanding of? Why (see p. 98)?

6. How did God reveal Himself in a general sense (Rom. 1:18-20)? What did man do with that revelation of truth (Rom. 1:18*b*, 25*a*; see p. 98)?

7. Why can't God be worshiped apart from His written revelation (see p. 98)?

8. Worshiping is an expression of _____ from the depth of the heart toward a God who is understood through His _____ (Ps. 47:7; see p. 98).

105

9. Why is expository preaching important from the standpoint of worship (see p. 99)?

10. What was the substance of truth upon which the early church worshiped (Acts 2:42; see p. 99)?

11. Why was the worship of the Athenians unacceptable (Acts 17:23; see p. 100)?

12. What are four results of worship (see pp. 100-101)?

13. Why is a worshiping church a pure church (see p. 100)?

14. Why is the Lord's Table so important in the worship of the church (see p. 101)?

15. Explain the statement "True worship changes people" (see p. 101).

16. What can have a greater impact than a single sermon (see p. 101)?

17. What are the four checkpoints to determine whether you are properly prepared for worship (Heb. 10:22; see pp. 102-3)?

18. Identify some barriers to worship. Give some scriptural examples of men who overcame them (see pp. 104-5).

19. How was David able to worship in the midst of divine chastening (see p. 104)?

Pondering the Principles

1. If we are to worship God, we must understand who He is. Most people will admit to belief in a superior being, but often they will have their own self-styled concept of who He is. How would you go about trying to direct someone from his own subjective speculations about God to the truth of the Bible? Consider the following approach: Ask him how he knows what God is like and how God demands to be worshiped. If he will agree that God has revealed Himself, ask him where He has been more fully revealed than in the Bible. Demonstrate that it claims to be an objective source of truth (Ps. 119:160; John 17:17), but that men have rejected truth (Rom. 1:18-25, 28, 32). Determine if he thinks it is logical to worship in ignorance, regardless of how sincere he may be (Acts 17:23). Assuming that he recognizes that the worship of an almighty being is a serious issue, ask him if he is willing to pay the consequences if, after a life of self-styled worship, he were to discover that his worship had been unacceptable to God. Share with him the consequences delineated in Scripture for rejecting the truth (John 8:24; 14:6; 2 Thess. 1:7-10; 2:8-12). Stress that his eternal destiny rests on whether he has offered acceptable or unacceptable worship. Make sure he knows that Christ offers eternal life to those who believe in Him (John 3:16-18; 17:3). Don't forget to pray that the Spirit would open his blinded eyes and to keep the doors open for future discussions with him (2 Tim. 2:24-26).

2. Are you preparing for worship any differently than before, now that you have completed this book? Before you worship on Sunday, go through the four checkpoints listed in reference to Hebrews 10:22. Are you worshiping God with your whole heart? Are you trusting in the truth revealed in the New Testament for your salvation? Do you come to God in humility,

recognizing that you are unworthy to enter His presence apart from the righteousness bestowed on you through Christ's death? Are you constantly confessing your sin as the Spirit convicts you of it? Lastly, are there any barriers of bitterness from chastening, or difficult circumstances, or of apathy that are preventing you from worshiping God in spirit and in truth? If so, strive to resolve them that your worship might be acceptable to God.

Moody Press, a ministry of the Moody Bible Institute, is designed for education, evangelization, and edification. If we may assist you in knowing more about Christ and the Christian life, please write us without obligation: Moody Press, c/o MLM, Chicago, IL 60610.